C000294711

# *The Daily Companion*

Elizabeth Rundle

Marshall Pickering

Marshall Morgan and Scott
Marshall Pickering
34–42 Cleveland Street, London W1P 5FB, UK

Copyright © 1989 Elizabeth Rundle
First published in 1989 by Marshall Morgan and Scott Publications Ltd
Part of the Marshall Pickering Holdings Group

All rights reserved. No part of this publication may be reproduced, stored
in a retrieval system, or transmitted, in any form or by any means, electronic
mechanical, photocopying, recording or otherwise, without the permission
in writing, of the publisher.

Scripture quotations in this publication include
extracts from the Holy Bible, New International Version.
Copyright © 1973, 1978, 1984 International Bible Society.

ISBN: 0 551 01883 6

Text set in Baskerville by Input Typesetting Ltd, London
Printed in Great Britain by Courier International Ltd, Tiptree, Colchester

*About the compiler:*

Born in London in 1948, Elizabeth Rundle lives in Cornwall. She contributes to local religious radio and television programmes and has written for a variety of Christian magazines. She is a local preacher within the Methodist church and enjoys amongst a wide range of interests, music, cricket, travel and people.

# To my friends

who supported and cared for me on the death of my beloved husband. To pluralise Ecclesiasticus 6:15 – 'Faithful friends are beyond price.'

# 1st January

He who was seated in the throne said: 'Behold, I am making all things new'.

Revelation 21:5

*Give us through the coming year*
*Quietness of mind,*
*Teach us to be patient*
*And always to be kind . . .*
*Give us reassurance*
*When everything goes wrong,*
*So our faith remains unfaltering*
*And our hope and courage strong . . .*
*And show us that in quietness*
*We can feel your presence near,*
*Filling us with joy and peace*
*Throughout the coming year.*

*Helen Steiner Rice*

A New Year! Lord I can't help but tremble a little at the year spread before me – teach me to fill each day with twenty four hours of love . . . and to so live that I can say, 'Not I, but Christ within me'.

* * *

# 2nd January

If I go up to the heavens, You are there, if I make my bed in the depths, You are there . . . if I settle on the far side of the sea, even there Your hand will guide me . . .

Psalm 139:8.9

This year I shall make a great effort to keep in mind the experience of the psalmist – God my Father has promised that there is nowhere and no time that He cannot be found. There is nothing I shall have to face, no operation, no sad parting, no anxiety but He is ever present by His spirit to guide me, uphold me and comfort me. In the hell of a breaking marriage, in seemingly insoluble problems with in-laws – in the good and the bad times, Lord, breathe Your hope into my heart.

*There is no place where God is not*
*Wherever I go, there God is.*
*Now and always He upholds me with His power*
*And keeps me safe in His love.*

*Scripture Union*

* * *

# 3rd January

Let us hold unswervingly to the hope we profess, for He who promised is faithful.

Hebrews 10:23

There come times in life when we feel the ground has been taken from under our feet . . . when we feel so emotionally and spiritually punched, that is the time when we need something to hold on to – a kind of 'handrail of faith' for the uphill climb. If you feel like that today put your hand out to Jesus – He knows the individual need, He turned even to the anonymous little woman who crept to touch the hem of His clothing . . . so, don't be afraid, He has time for you . . . He has time and love and peace of mind for all who reach out and hold on unswervingly.

*Will your anchor hold in the storms of life?*
*We have an anchor that keeps the soul*
*Steadfast and sure while the billows roll*
*Fastened to the rock which cannot move –*
*Grounded firm and deep in the Saviour's love.*

*Priscilla Owens*

* * *

# 4th January

Praise be to the God and Father of our Lord Jesus Christ! In His great mercy He has given us new birth . . .

1 Peter 1:3

A birth brings about complete change for both parents and baby – baby is suddenly thrust from the dark safety of the womb into 'life' and life is never the same for parents again! Yet have you ever thought that there are three kinds of birth we can experience? We all have the natural birth but then after months (perhaps years) of generally disrupting everyone else around, bawling for feeds, etc, we grow to a moral birth when we naturally take into consideration the needs and wishes of others. We learn the meaning of 'don't, because . . .' For the Christian there is the third spiritual birth. And just like the other two, the third birth entails a complete change – no longer just life but Life in all its fullness and peace with joy in the knowledge of sins forgiven.

*Jesus replied to Nicodemus: 'I tell you the truth, unless a man is born again, he cannot see the kingdom of God.'*

*John 3:3*

*'Flesh gives birth to flesh, but the Spirit gives birth to spirit.'*

*John 3:6*

* * *

# 5th January

Prepare the way for the Lord – make straight paths for Him.

Matthew 3:3

I must set out upon the road that leads to God. The one necessity for that journey is that the road must be open – that it must not be a blind alley or blocked by insurmountable obstructions. But that necessity has already been attended to; the road is clear, and it will never be blocked. I am certain of this truth, because not even Calvary was able to shut this road for Jesus. Even in the throes of this unique test, Jesus was able to make His unfaltering way along it. And now and always He keeps it open for me and for all doubting sinners.

Lord Soper

*O for a closer walk with God*
*A calm and heavenly frame,*
*A light to shine upon the road*
*That leads me to the Lamb.*

*William Cowper*

* * *

# 6th January

Peter asked: 'Lord, Why can't I follow You now?'

John 13:37

Peter was so uninhibited in his enthusiasm – so normal in his reactions, we all echo the desire to know 'why' and we don't want to wait, we want to know 'now'. I can almost feel the patience in the gaze of Jesus as he looked on Peter – and I'm impetuous too, Lord: I plunge into things expecting instant results, immediate answers; long-term commitments puzzle me. I need to learn Your patience to understand that things happen in Your good time, not mine. But it is hard, Lord. Why can't there be peace in the world today? Why can't Christians find unity now? Why is there never a perfect answer to anything? As I calm my mind for a few moments, come to me in peace. . . . I have no answers except God is good.

*Why restless, why cast down my soul?*
*Hope still and thou shalt sing*
*The praise of Him who is thy God*
*And health's eternal spring.*

*Tate & Brady*

* * *

# 7th January

This is the account of the heavens and the earth when they were created:

When the Lord God made the earth and the heavens, no shrub of the field had yet appeared on the earth and no plant of the field had yet sprung up; the Lord God had not sent rain on the earth, and there was no man to work the ground, but streams came up from the earth and watered the whole surface of the ground. And the Lord God formed man from the dust of the ground and breathed into his nostrils the breath of life, and the man became a living being.

Now the Lord God had planted a garden in the east, in Eden; and there he put the man he had formed. And the Lord God made all kinds of trees grow out of the ground – trees that were pleasing to the eye and good for food.

In the middle of the garden were the tree of life and the tree of knowledge of good and evil.

Genesis 2:4–9

* * *

# 8th January

Man is born to trouble as surely as sparks fly upward.

Job 5:7

So much of a tragic nature happens that it is all too easy to slip into the gloomy, fatalistic approach, and some people appear to have trouble heaped in their direction. One of the more tragic events is the death of a child. The shock of finding a baby dead can only be understood by parents who have similarly suffered. Before her tiny son died, Carole had not heard of the Cot Death Research Fund, but since joining the local group she has been able to talk out the shared agony with other parents. The group generally comforts each other in the realisation that they are not isolated in their grief. Trouble can be worked through and personal heartache is a means to reach others in despair – to offer hope, direction and sympathy. Trouble will always be in the world, but praise God, through all He is with us.

*Lord God, I pray for bereaved parents, guide those who will counsel and comfort them, and out of their hot tears may life and love be enriched in Your name.*

* * *

# 9th January

Jesus said: 'Father into thy hands I commit my spirit. . . .'

Luke 23:46

*Father I place into Your hands*
*The things that I can't do.*
*Father I place into Your hands*
*The times that I've been through.*
*Father I place into Your hands*
*The way that I should go,*
*For I know I always can trust You.*

*Father, I place into Your hands*
*My friends and family.*
*Father I place into Your hands*
*The things that trouble me.*
*Father I place into Your hands*
*The person I would be,*
*For I know I always can trust You.*

*J. Hewer*

Lord into Your hands we commit Your universal Church, and her unity. Into Your hands we commit all the problems which seem insoluble, in sure and certain hope, for we trust You. Here and now we leave all in Your hands.

* * *

# 10th January

May the God of peace, who through the blood of the eternal covenant brought back from the dead our Lord Jesus . . . equip you with everything good for doing His will. . . .

Hebrews 13:20

This 'Preshana' is taken from the Church of South India Liturgy for celebrating the Lord's Supper:

*The God of peace will be with you*
*And grant you His peace at all times,*
*Peace beyond our understanding*
*That purifies heart, mind and body*
*Until His Kingdom comes. Amen*
*Having shared the feast of God's love,*
*Go into the world to share His love in your life.*

In pity look upon thy children's striving for life and freedom, peace and brotherhood: Till, at the fullness of thy truth arriving, we find in Christ the crown of every good.

Albert F. Bayly

* * *

# 11th January

. . . since the day we heard about you, we have not stopped praying for you and asking God to fill you with the knowledge of His will . . .

Colossians 1:9

The late Dr William Barclay was a genius in making nuggets of theology plain – even blunt. He brushed away pious mists and jolted people into thinking again, and thinking for themselves. So often I ramble on in prayer with all the pressing needs in my heart, totally carried away with my idea of what I'm praying for – Oh, the truth of Barclay's words: 'We are apt to think that prayer is asking God for what we want when true prayer is asking God what He wants!' Lord, wake me to the needs of others . . . shake me to urgency in prayer . . . break me from self . . . make me more like Jesus.

*Praying for others will always be a demanding experience. It means that we put ourselves in their position, feel their pain, explore their dilemma. And then stand with them and plead for them in the light and warmth of God's love.*

*Joyce Upton*

* * *

# 12th January

We tell you the good news!

Acts 13:32

Real hope is not just based on wishful thinking. Jesus Christ came into this world, sharing in its sufferings and leading us back to God – this is Good News. We can be given strength not to ignore sufferings but do something to help. Caring for the homeless, the addict, the lonely and those under emotional stress may not be newsworthy but its good news to those in need.

Sandy Gall speaking about the Church Army

*Then let the servant church arise,*
*A caring church that longs to be*
*A partner in Christ's sacrifice,*
*And clothed in Christ's humanity.*

*F. Pratt Green*

* * *

# 13th January

Jesus said: 'The kingdom of God does not come visibly, nor will people say "here it is" or "there it is", because the kingdom of God is within you.'

Luke 17:21

High-powered telescopes probe billions of miles into outer space yet no heaven is revealed. It's too easy to hang on to the simple Victorian imagery of heaven as being 'above the clear blue sky' – we cannot explain it when asked so we tend to skirt the truth.

And all the while we have the truth confronting us from the gospels in the words of Jesus. Lord, open my mind to know that I don't find heaven by straining and calculating, by testing and searching – You and Your heaven can live within me, in depths that I myself am hardly aware of . . . Lord, breathe the peace of Your kingdom into my soul.

*Thy kingdom come – on earth as it is in heaven.*
*Thy will be done – on earth as it is in heaven:*
*Give us the daily bread of heaven –*
*Join us with the loved ones in heaven:*
*Infuse us with the love of heaven in our lives.*

* * *

# 14th January

Now Abel kept flocks, and Cain worked the soil. In the course of time Cain brought some of the fruits of the soil as an offering to the Lord. But Abel brought fat portions from some of the firstborn of his flock. The Lord looked with favour on Abel and his offering, but on Cain and his offering He did not look with favour. So Cain was very angry, and his face was downcast. Then the Lord said to Cain, 'Why are you angry? Why is your face downcast? If you do what is right, will you not be accepted? But if you do not do what is right, sin is crouching at your door; it desires to have you, but you must master it.'

Now Cain said to his brother Abel, 'Let's go out to the field.' And while they were in the field, Cain attacked his brother Abel and killed him.

Then the Lord said to Cain, 'Where is your brother Abel?' 'I don't know,' he replied. 'Am I my brother's keeper?'

The Lord said, 'What have you done?'

Genesis 4:2–10

* * *

# 15th January

'May the lord pay no attention to that wicked man Nabal. He is just like his name – his name is Fool and folly goes with him.'

1 Samuel 25:25

And so brave Abigail made her effort as peacemaker before the furious King David. Her husband Nabal had refused David and his men even the meanest of refreshment but Abigail, realising that it was not a good thing to annoy a hungry army, quickly went without Nabal's knowing to apologise to King David.

An ancient tale of a long-suffering wife picking up the pieces to make the best of a poor situation. Today I pray for wives stoically coping with their husbands drinking, brutality and stubborness. May the gracious spirit of Abigail rest on them.

*When David heard that Nabal was dead . . . he sent word to Abigail, asking her to become his wife. She bowed down her face to the ground and said: 'Here is your maidservant, ready to serve you.'*

*1 Samuel 25:40–41*

* * *

# 16th January

All men are like grass, and all their glory is like the flowers of the field. The grass withers and the flowers fall . . .

Isaiah 40:7

The story is told of how one day Queen Elizabeth I looked into her mirror and recoiled at the reflection. She was not growing old gracefully – and in her regal horror she banned all mirrors from her palaces. It sounds more like the tantrum of an ageing movie-star than a shrewd, revered Queen, but it underlines the fact that Queen or not, she could not stop Time. Lord, help me to face ageing, not to be vain or afraid or even to despise age but to get on with living each day and thank You for the certain calmness that maturity brings . . . and also, Lord, when I do catch a glimpse of myself in the mirror, remind me that I can remain young at heart!

*When the flower of youth has faded,*
*When frail of limb and dim of eye*
*I kneel to worship, take my praises*
*Leaving earth to thrill the sky.*

* * *

# 17th January

Then Peter came to Jesus and asked, 'Lord, how many times shall I forgive my brother . . . ?'
Matthew 18:21

Reconciliation. Oh, the thousands of hurting people in families, in work places, in churches, in politics, in streets, in marriages . . . Pride forbids them from outwardly admitting their need for reconciliation, and the wounds fester on to despair. In the rebuilt Coventry Cathedral, the Friday noon litany includes the words: 'Be kind to one another, tender-hearted, forgiving one another as God in Christ forgave you'. Lord help me to be kind, tender and forgiving today – and may those who are embittered be melted by Your forgiving love.

*How can Your pardon reach and bless the unforgiving heart*
*That broods on wrongs, and will not let old bitterness depart?*
*Lord, cleanse the depths within our souls, and bid resentment cease;*
*Then, reconciled to God and man our lives will spread Your peace.*
*Rosamond E. Herklots*

* * *

# 18th January

But if we walk in the light, as He is in the light, we have fellowship with one another and the blood of Jesus, His son, purifies us from every sin.

1 John 1:7

The characters whom we meet in the pages of the New Testament and who first heard the claims of the Master do not belong to a species bearing only faint resemblance to the folk who live in your street. The world is still peopled by Peters and Johns and Marthas and Marys. In fact, the first disciples are far more contemporary figures than the nebulous creatures depicted in the modern novel as being 'modern Types'. If then, the Christian life is the way in which God's children ought to walk in every age and along every road, then what was 'Good News' for Saul of Tarsus is equally 'Good News' for you and me.

Lord Soper

*Walk in the Light; so shalt thou know*
*That fellowship of love*
*His spirit only can bestow*
*Who reigns in Light above.*

*Bernard Barton*

* * *

# 19th January

Now may the Lord of peace Himself give you peace at all times and in every way. The Lord be with you all.

2 Thessalonians 3:16

Fashions change, pop songs are all the rage one day then lie unloved for twenty years or so to be revamped and popular once more. Forms of worship change, language changes to suit the generation . . . yet within all this atmosphere of change there is the insatiable desire for unchanging truth. All through the centuries people have turned to Jesus, the Life, the Truth and the Way . . . Today, Lord, I repeat a 9th Century blessing and marvel at how real the blessing has been to countless Christians in every age and situation.

*May God the Father bless us,*
*May Christ the Son take care of us,*
*The Holy Ghost enjoy thanks all the days of our life.*
*The Lord be our defender and keeper of body and soul*
*Both now and for ever. Amen*

*Bishop Aedelward (9th century)*

* * *

# 20th January

He reveals the deep things of darkness and brings deep shadows into the light . . . they grope in darkness with no light.

Job 12:22–24

In my teens, each morning began at ten to six when I braved the dark winter mornings with a hurricane lamp and trudged to the cowshed to milk the two cows. When all around is darkness, a light, however small, is a comfort and once in the cowshed the electric light seemed to give warmth as well. Looking over the valley I would see other lights denoting other people were up and beginning their chores too. Unspoken, anonymous companionship. City lights similarly tell us that others are around – so there's no need to feel isolated . . . others too face the day with all the same niggles and uncertainties . . . others too long to home in on the light of Love, to know they belong to God and all will be well.

*Much of our faith comes through groping, and sensing, and feeling. And when God is ready he lets us turn on the light which reveals Him.*

*Jeremy Dowling*

* * *

## 21st January

Jacob left Beersheba and set out for Haran. When he reached a certain place, he stopped for the night because the sun had set. Taking one of the stones there he put it under his head and lay down to sleep. He had a dream in which he saw a stairway resting on the earth, with its top reaching to heaven, and the angels of God were ascending and descending. There above it stood the Lord, and He said 'I am the Lord, the God of your father Abraham and the God of Isaac. I will give you and your descendants the land on which you are lying. Your descendants will be like the dust of the earth, and you will spread out to the west and to the east, to the north and to the south. All peoples will be blessed through you and your offspring. I am with you and will watch over you wherever you go, and I will bring you back to this land. I will not leave you until I have done what I have promised you.'

When Jacob awoke from his sleep, he thought, 'Surely, the Lord is in this place, and I was not aware of it.'

Genesis 28:10–16

* * *

## 22nd January

. . . His compassions never fail. They are new every morning . . .

Lamentations 3:23

On a Monday morning many new things are likely to happen. Some people are starting new jobs, and others are adjusting to the new freedom of retirement. Couples are beginning their first week of married life together, and other families are enjoying the new excitement of a baby in their midst. For many, this week will be the start of a new life without their partner or a loved one – all new experiences that one way or another we are not ever truly prepared for. Lord, I pray that in all my ups and all my downs I will remember that when things and people in the world change, Your love and guidance never changes – it comes to me new and fresh every morning. From the bottom of my heart – thank You.

*Every day that goes by shows Your mercy,*
*And every gift that You give shows You care:*
*Every song that I sing says You're worthy*
*And I will bless Your holy name.*

*Eddie Espinosa*

* * *

# 23rd January

Jesus told them: 'The harvest is plentiful, but the workers are few.'

Luke 10:2

*There's a work for Jesus*
*Ready at your hand:*
*'Tis a task the Master*
*Just for you has planned.*

*Haste to do His bidding*
*Yield your service true,*
*There's a work for Jesus*
*None but you can do!*

*Anon*

Forgive me, Lord, that I shirk from or put off things I know I can do, and ought to do – I wait for someone else to take responsibility, then I find fault when things go wrong or get left undone. I need to buck up my ideas – I need to realise my Master is just waiting for me to get a move on . . .

* * *

# 24th January

> See, they will come from afar – some from the north, some from the west, some from the region of Sinim . . .
>
> Isaiah 49:12

Many families are spread all around the world today. Sons, daughters, parents, grandchildren – separated by thousands of miles. Lord, you know the inner heartache of such separation – you feel the anguish for your children. I pray that Your love will protect my loved ones wherever they are. And may Your love be that invisible chain which links us together no matter how many miles come between. I rest all my thoughts and concerns at the throne of eternal grace and go on my daily round comforted.

*Coming, coming, yes they are coming from afar*
*All to meet in plains of glory*
*All to sing His praises sweet;*
*What a chorus, what a meeting,*
*With the family complete!*

*J. Wakefield MacGill*

* * *

# 25th January

> Men of Israel, listen to this: Jesus of Nazareth was a man accredited by God to you by miracles, wonders and signs.
>
> Acts 2:22

When Win was diagnosed as having an inoperable brain tumour, and given only weeks to live, all her friends prayed desperately for a miracle. In spite of all the prayers Win deteriorated fast and died. Her husband, family and friends had prayed for the miracle of healing, but God did indeed work a miracle – a miracle of witness. Win's faith became a talking point: the holding of hands in prayer around her bed became an uplifting blessing; her rock-solid trust in her living Saviour was an unforgettable inspiration. Win had won the victory and touched countless heart with her heart ablaze for Christ.

*Jesus said: 'Because I live, you also will live.' Lord, I open my heart to claim the miracle of everlasting love and life.*

* * *

# 26th January

> Jesus said: 'I have come that they may have life, and have it to the full'.
>
> John 10:10

In order that God's children of all races, creeds and colours may have this full life, each one needs to be loved. This is what Jesus came to show during His life on earth: for He is love. And there is so much in our surroundings here that is truly beautiful that we are constantly reminded of this love; the loving thoughtfulness of a colleague who understands when one is struggling to adjust to a very difficult climate; the beauty of nature as the grass, fresh green leaves and vivid colours of flowers and shrubs spring to new life after the fall of rain; the shy smile of a little child who offers her hand in greeting. All these make one grateful to God to be alive and to be given health, strength and opportunity to share with colleagues in an unfamiliar part of His world and to be used in some small way as a channel for His love.

June Walker
(formerly served in Kenya)

*Life and light and joy are found in the presence of the Lord!*
*Charles E. Mudie*

* * *

# 27th January

Then he (the Samaritan) put the man on his own donkey, brought him to an inn and took care of him.

Luke 10:34

So many people need to be cared for today – the physically and the mentally handicapped, the very young, the very old and the thousands suffering from debilitating diseases or the result of accidents. They are so easy to forget as I plough through the busy things of each day, yet mothers and wives give most of their lives in 'caring': in unknown streets, behind front doors, devotion mingles with frustration, progress and set-backs are the highs and lows of experience, triumphs and sorrow merge with the heartbeat of the city. The Samaritan was unknown – the man set upon by thieves was anonymous also – yet the need for love and care was as essential to that individual as to all the individuals who this day will be loved and cared for.

*Loving heavenly Father, bless those who care with Your patience, when helplessness gives way to resentment and repeated demands exhaust and exasperate, fill the room with Your peace, may Christ's example encourage gentleness and the supporting prayers of friends translate duty into a beautiful act of love.*

* * *

# 28th January

Then God said to Noah, 'Come out of the ark, you and your wife, and your sons and their wives. Bring out every kind of living creature that is with you – the birds, the animals, and all the creatures that move along the ground – so they can multiply on the earth and be fruitful and increase in number upon it.'

So Noah came out, together with his sons and his wife and his sons' wives. All the animals and all the creatures that move along the ground and all the birds – everything that moves on the earth – came out of the ark, one kind after another.

Then Noah built an altar to the Lord and, taking some of all the clean animals and clean birds, he sacrificed burnt offerings on it. The Lord smelled the pleasing aroma and said in His heart . . .

*As long as the earth endures,*
*Seedtime and harvest, cold and heat,*
*Summer and winter,*
*Day and night*
*Will never cease.*

*Genesis 8:15–22*

* * *

# 29th January

Jesus prayed: 'My prayer is not for them alone. I pray also for those who will believe in me through their message . . .'

John 17:20

On the outside it may seem that no one in your office is interested in God – but if you could somehow see into the hearts and minds of your co-workers you would probably be very surprised.

All around you are people who are spiritually needy, and God wants to use you to tell them about Christ who alone can meet their deepest needs.

How can you witness for Christ? First, pray by name for those around you. Only God can prepare their hearts to receive the Gospel. Pray for yourself also, that God will give you a deeper love for them.

Billy Graham

*Lord God, I pray today for . . . and . . . guide me and give me a listening ear, a calm, sympathetic nature and Your words of encouragement for those with whom I work.*

* * *

# 30th January

Rejoice that you participate in the sufferings of Christ, so that you may be overjoyed when His glory is revealed.

1 Peter 4:13

This is a quote from a very sick lady who nevertheless gives her prayer life to pray for others: 'I had a very rich spiritual experience at the beginning of this year and the experience lives on in me. It was at the hospital while they were giving me my pacemaker and I was in the intensive care unit. I was aware of my smallness, of my weakness, of my wretchedness, but also of the infinite greatness of God . . . of His paternal love . . .

I remain very restricted in what I can do and very tired, but I have my finger on the true value of life – the sheer greatness of life.'

*There is a tremendous strength that is growing in the world through this continual sharing together, praying together, suffering together and working together.*

*Mother Teresa*

* * *

# 31st January

One thing I ask of the Lord . . . that I may dwell in the house of the Lord all the days of my life, to gaze upon the beauty of the Lord and to seek Him in His temple.

Psalm 27:4

Benjamin Waugh was a young congregational minister when he moved to London and came face to face with Dickensian poverty and social squalor. Most of us are temporarily moved by sights of children, especially those who are undernourished, dressed in rags and homeless . . . mostly the sights are of far away and we quite soon fill our minds with better things. However, Benjamin Waugh could not forget the plight of the children he had seen and his faith turned to deeds as he helped to found an organisation to help abandoned boys take up a career at sea. He was also one of the founders of the N.S.P.C.C. and retired early to devote the rest of his life to 'the children'.

*Now let us see Thy beauty Lord*
*As we have seen before:*
*And by Thy beauty quicken us*
*To love Thee and adore.*

*Benjamin Waugh*

* * *

# 1st February

Jesus said: 'Lo, I am with you always . . .'

Matthew 28:20

There are times when I don't feel that 'presence' – I feel cut-off, spare, uncertain and without any particular purpose . . . Why do I get these feelings? – surely others must feel the same –.

When I take up the Bible, I read of many people who seemed inclined to moodiness, too, Moses, Jacob, Job, Hosea . . . and reading about other people it is easy to see how God was with them even when they weren't aware of Him. Oh, that today, in my life, I may grasp the reality for myself . . .

*Lord Jesus, guard and guide me through the hours, days, weeks, months and years ahead, that I may do Your will, glorify my Father in heaven, fulfil my obligations to my fellow men and love my neighbour as myself.*

*Prayer From St Wilfrid's, Harehills*

* * *

# 2nd February

> Then Miriam the prophetess, Aaron's sister, took a tambourine in her hand, and all the women followed her, with tambourines and dancing.
>
> Exodus 15:20

In fiction, family 'sagas' always attract a high level of interest, and it seems we all like to know how people get on through life. In the Bible, alongside the story of Moses, we can trace the life of his big sister from the young girl, who stood tentatively by the banks of the Nile watching to see what would happen to her baby brother, to the influential prophetess leading the singing and dancing. The demure maiden grew into a woman of passions who witnessed triumphs and also adversity – to a degree, that happens to us all as we grow up . . . Oh Lord, I look at the life of Miriam and see the dangers of jealousy and quick temper, but also I see the spontaneity of praising God – singing – dancing in worshipful joy.

*I danced in the morning when the world was begun*
*I danced in the moon and the stars and the sun . . .*
*Dance then wherever you may be*
*I am the Lord of the Dance, said he*
*And I'll lead you all wherever you may be*
*And I'll lead you all in the dance said he.*

*Sydney Carter*

* * *

# 3rd February

> Why are you downcast, O my soul? . . . Put your hope in God, for I will yet praise Him, my Saviour and my God.
>
> Psalm 42:5

Usually we think we deserve a 'little fun' by a fling into sinning when life has handed us some injustice or when we have stuck faithfully through some protracted trial . . . Many of us have found out what a deadly brew this is. Our eyes are completely off Christ and on ourselves . . . Out of this little mess, Satan has worked some great triumphs. But what if we are already in the middle of such a mess? What if one's life is snarled up by bad human relationships, fears that one can't get rid of, debts, illness? Is there any hope? There certainly is! That's precisely the good news Christ brings us . . .

Catherine Marshall

*For what is our hope, our joy, or the crown in which we will glory in the presence of our Lord Jesus Christ when He comes? Is it not you? Indeed, You are our glory and joy.*

*1 Thessalonians 2:19*

* * *

# 4th February

When you have eaten and are satisfied, praise the Lord your God for the good land He has given you. Be careful that you do not forget the Lord your God, failing to observe his commands, his laws and his decrees that I am giving you today. Otherwise, when you eat and are satisfied when you build fine houses and settle down, and when your herds and flocks grow large and your silver and gold increase and all you have is multiplied, then will your heart become proud and you will forget the Lord your God . . . You may say to yourself, 'My power and the strength of my hands have produced this wealth for me.'

But remember the Lord your God, for it is He who gives you the ability to produce wealth.

Deuteronomy 8:10–18

* * *

# 5th February

Someone in the crowd said to Jesus, 'Teacher, tell my brother to divide the inheritance with me.'

Luke 12:13

O Lord, tell those people to stop squabbling! Lord, tell my child to stop gambling . . . Lord, tell that family to bury their grievances . . . Lord, tell – Yes, it's easy to see others always in the wrong and to expect emotional messes to be sorted out by the Lord. But what about me? What do I need telling? I'm not as perfect as I try to make out – I need to look at myself first, get myself sorted out, long before I look at others. I need to reread the passages in the Gospel and understand that one of the greatest pitfalls for a disciple of Jesus is to imagine He is speaking about other people. Open my eyes, Lord, open my ears . . . open my soul to Your voice.

*Talk with us, Lord, Thyself reveal –*
*Thou callest me to seek Thy face*
*'Tis all I wish to seek;*
*To attend the whispers of They grace*
*And hear Thee only speak.*

*Charles Wesley*

* * *

# 6th February

Though the doors were locked, Jesus came and stood among them, and said, 'Peace be with you!'

John 20:26

His presence is meant to be real to us, all the time and everywhere, especially when we are bearing our witness to Him, or are suffering for His sake, or are in trouble of any kind. But with all too many of us the realisation of His presence is intermittent, fluctuating, indistinct, unsatisfying. What a pity this is! When we lack the consciousness of

His presence we are easily disturbed, disheartened, ruffled, impatient, wrongly self-assertive, but when we live in the joyful comfort of His realised presence we become optimistic amid discouragements, patient amid tribulation, brave amid danger, calm amid strife, cheerful amid monotony.

J. Sidlow-Baxter

*Jesus said: 'Because I live, you also will live. On that day you will realise that I am in my Father and you in me, and I in you.'*

*John 14:20*

* * *

# 7th February

> Offer hospitality to one another without grumbling. Each one should use whatever gift he has received to serve others, faithfully administering God's grace in its various forms.
>
> 1 Peter 4:9

Have you ever been scuttling around preparing for guests and all the time wishing they had not been invited? Perhaps we can imagine some wife of an early Christian household wringing her hands and sighing: 'Not another apostle coming to stay!' Peter had obviously come up against this grudging welcome. But how comforting and uplifting it is to receive a warm and genuine welcome . . . and each one in the household can add their own gift to add to that hospitality. Lord, I don't want people to grumble when I appear – give me Your grace to open my home . . . to receive anyone as I would wish to be received.

*But at the coming of the King of Heaven*
*We're caught all at six and seven . . .*
*We entertain Him always like a stranger*
*And, as at first, still lodge Him in the manger.*

*Anon*

* * *

# 8th February

God loves a cheerful giver. And God is able to make all grace abound in you.

2 Corinthians 9:7

When the alarm goes I cannot say I'm cheerful. I'm not filled with a good grace when I look at a pile of dishes in the sink or a line full of washing that the rain has just 'washed' again. Yet, even though I'm not giving to other people a slice of my ill-humour, I'm giving it to myself. Lord, I pray for good grace, for cheerfulness and a sense of pleasantness and warm humour – of course I don't want people to think I'm a sour puss, so I'll give a wave, a smile, my listening ear – help me to give of myself to others through Your grace in Your love.

*The day returns and brings us the petty round of irritating concerns and duties . . . help us to perform them with laughter and kind faces, let cheerfulness abound with industry. Bring us to our beds weary and content and undishonoured, and grant us in the end the gift of sleep.*

*R. L. Stevenson*

* * *

# 9th February

And Tamar took the bread she had prepared and brought it to her brother Amnon in his bedroom.

2 Samuel 13:10

The biblical story of Tamar's rape, the incestuous act which ruined her life, has its echo down the centuries and across the world. Women are distraught, humiliated and violated today. Lord, I cannot shut my eyes to this violent truth just because I find it distasteful or hard to believe – help me not to judge, enable me to love in Jesus' name and pray for the new life that can be theirs when they return to the Saviour. Poor Tamar's despair led to her brother committing murder . . . one sin leads to another and another . . . the evil spiral has a suffocating hold; but today's victim can live again in the pure, cleansing love of Christ Jesus.

*I was so lost – but You showed me the way*
*'Cause you are the way:*
*I was lied to – but You told me the truth,*
*'Cause You are the truth:*

*Keith Green*

* * *

# 10th February

Joseph said: 'Do not be distressed and do not be angry with yourselves for selling me here . . . so then, it was not you who sent me here, but God.'

Genesis 45:5–8

What a large heart Joseph had – after being unceremoniously bundled off into Egypt we would expect him to blow his top at the sight of his wretched brothers again. But no, Joseph had learned that God had a plan for his life and His plan was greater than any underhanded trading of his brothers. Joseph had learnt that God's purpose could not be hindered and whatever happened was for His glory. Afraid I haven't got that largeness of heart – yet.

*God is at work in us*
*His purpose to perform*
*Building a kingdom*
*Of power not of words,*
*Where things impossible*
*By faith shall be made possible:*
*Let's give the glory to Him now.*

*Graham Kendrick*

* * *

## 11th February

And now, O Israel, what does the Lord your God ask of you but to fear the Lord your God, to walk in all His ways, to love Him, to serve the Lord your God with all your heart and with all your soul, and to observe the Lord's commands and decrees that I am giving you today for your own good.

To the Lord your God belong the heavens, even the highest heavens, the earth and everything in it. Yet the Lord set His affection on your forefathers and loved them, and He chose you, their descendants, above all the nations, as it is today. Circumcise your hearts, therefore, and do not be stiff-necked any longer. For the Lord your God is God of gods and Lord of lords, the great God, mighty and awesome, who shows no partiality and accepts no bribes. He defends the cause of the fatherless and the widow, and loves the alien, giving him food and clothing. And you are to love those who are aliens for you yourselves were aliens in Egypt.

Fear the Lord your God and serve Him.

Deuteronomy 10:12–20

* * *

## 12th February

Then the man said: 'Lord, I believe', and he worshipped Him.

John 9:38

The undeniable agony in the world is used by many to say they cannot believe in God. Yet it is a paradox that those who see the depth of spiritual and physical anguish are those who have experienced a greater quality of spirit and greatness of heart, and will say most definitely that they believe in God. Mother Frances Dominica, living with the strains of a children's hospice, put it this way: 'It's made

God very much more real for me – more times than I can count I have to say, I don't know, I don't understand but I do believe!'

*My God is so real*
*So loving and patient*
*And He loves me and you.*
*Creation is His and Kinship too*
*And all that is right and true:*
*My God is so real*
*So loving and patient*
*And He loves me and you.*

*Hannah, Kirsty, Claire, Ann and Kirsty S.*
*5 Sunday school children of 8/9*

* * *

# 13th February

Jesus said: 'All men will know that you are my disciples if you love one another.'

John 13:35

Carl Jung was counselling a man who had been receiving therapy for six months and was getting no better. Finally, Dr Jung said: 'Friend I cannot do any more for you. What you need is God.'

'How do I find God, Dr Jung?' the man asked.

'I don't know,' said Jung, 'but I suspect if you find a group of people that believe in Him passionately and just spend time with them – you will find God.'

*God forgave my sin in Jesus' name.*
*I've been born again in Jesus' name*
*And in Jesus' name I come to you*
*To share His love as He told me to:*
*He said 'Freely, freely you have received –*
*Freely, freely give:*
*Go in My name and because you believe,*
*Others will know that I live.'*

*Carol Owens*

* * *

# 14th February

Peace of mind makes the body healthy, but jealousy is like a cancer.

Proverbs 14:30 TEV

By tradition this is the most romantic day of the year! Even so, it is a day when many will feel wracked with jealousy instead of feeling the thrill of romance. Life is too short to spoil moments in dissatisfaction, whether it be for a wife or husband, the latest car or promotion. Protect me Lord from the creeping sin of jealousy – it means I'm concentrating on Myself . . . I need to open my mind to the needs and hopes of others for a change . . .

*Jealousy narrows a person Lord,*
*Makes his soul smaller . . . his character meaner,*
*It shrivels a person Lord, makes him less,*
*It sits on his shoulder like a vulture covered*
*in green slime, murmuring lies and obscenities,*
*with bad breath . . . Who needs it Lord?*

*David Kossoff*

* * *

# 15th February

While you were doing all these things, declares the Lord, I spoke to you again and again, but you didn't listen; I called you but you did not answer.

Jeremiah 7:13

Children will always hear the ice-cream van, always catch the position of their favourite pop group in the Top 40, but how unusually deaf they become when the call is 'bedtime'! The prophet Jeremiah spoke to the children of Israel in words we can all recognise . . . words of exasperation, underlying the old saying, 'There's none so deaf as those who won't hear'. Faults in the Israelite nation are obvious, faults in those around us stand out ripe for our criticism

Lord, restrain me from saying what people should do, and bring me in a moment of quiet, to be still and see my own shortcomings and at long last, listen to Your voice to me.

*Master speak and make me listen*
*Let me know it is to me.*

*F. R. Havergal*

* * *

# 16th February

And the Lord God commanded the man: 'You are free to eat from any tree in the garden, but you must not eat from the tree of knowledge of good and evil . . .

Genesis 2:16

A man was having a country cottage built and was confidant that the new garden would be ideal because he asked the advice of the old countryman who was to set it out. He told the old man to plant apple and walnut trees in certain places but was puzzled when he visited the garden and found the trees in different places.

'Well,' explained the gardener, 'I did think that when you and I are gone, then those walnut trees will shade them apple trees.'

Not many of us have the foresight to work out the long-term consequences of our actions . . . and it takes grace to allow that others sometimes know best . . . Lord, I'm trying to learn.

*Oh, Lord of the field and the garden*
*God of Wisdom and patience and thoughtfulness;*
*Help me to plant wisely the flowers of creation*
*And plant with more carefulness actions and words.*

* * *

# 17th February

By day the Lord went ahead of them in a pillar of cloud to guide them on their way . . .

Exodus 13:21

The most encouraging lesson to be taken for our day from the story of the Israelites' wander in the wilderness is to notice how God was with them, guiding them as a pillar of cloud by day and pillar of fire by night. In other words, day and night He guided them – they were never defenceless or alone. And those pillars of cloud and fire lasted for as long as the Israelites needed them. Lord, I feel in the wilderness quite often – and I'm prone to all the age-old weeping and wailing. Just make me be still for a minute and realise that Your power is undimmed and, day and night, in my own personal wilderness, You will guide me . . . always.

*Guide me O Thou great Redeemer*
*Pilgrim through this barren land;*
*I am weak, but Thou art mighty*
*Hold me with Thy powerful hand.*

*William Williams*

* * *

# 18th February

Celebrate the Feast of Tabernacles for seven days after you have gathered the produce of your threshing-floor and your wine-press. Be joyful at your feast – you, your sons and daughters, your menservants and maid-servants, and the Levites, the aliens, the fatherless and the widows who live in your towns. For seven days celebrate the Feast to the Lord your God at the place the Lord will choose. For the Lord your God will bless you in all your harvest and in all the work of your hands, and your joy will be complete.

Three times a year all your men must appear before the Lord your God at the place He will choose: at the Feast of Unleavened Bread, the Feast of Weeks and the Feast of Tabernacles.
No man should appear before the Lord empty-handed. Each of you must bring a gift in proportion to the way the Lord your God has blessed you.

Deuteronomy 16:13–17

* * *

# 19th February

Then I heard the voice of the Lord saying, 'Whom shall I send?' And I said, 'Here am I. Send me!'

Isaiah 6:8

There is too much truth in the old saying 'If you want something done – do it yourself!' So if we get irritated that no one seems willing to participate – everybody's get-up-and-go has got-up-and-gone – then how much more must our Lord be disappointed in us. Forgive me Lord that I am so ready to watch another do Your work, but so quick to exclaim when Your work is left undone . . . I know in my heart that You expect better things from me . . . help me, show me, inspire me.

*Here I am, Lord;*
*Here is my body – here is my heart – here is my soul.*
*Grant that I may be big enough to reach the world,*
*Strong enough to carry it,*
*Pure enough to embrace it without wanting to keep it.*

*Michael Quoist*

* * *

# 20th February

Jesus said: . . . 'he who seeks finds, and to him who knocks the door will be opened.'

Matthew 7:8

*I got up early one morning and rushed right into the day;*
*I had so much to accomplish that I didn't have time to pray.*
*Problems just tumbled about me, and heavier came each task.*
*'Why doesn't God help me?' I wondered.*
*He answered, 'You didn't ask!'*

*I wanted to see joy and beauty – but the day toiled on*
*Grey and bleak, I wondered why God didn't show me.*
*He said, 'But you didn't seek.'*

*I tried to come into God's presence;*
*I used all my keys at the lock.*
*God gently and lovingly chided,*
*'My child, you didn't knock.'*

*I woke up early this morning and paused before entering the day;*
*I had so much to accomplish that I had to take time to pray.*

*Unknown*

*Here I am. I stand at the door and knock.*

*Revelation 3:20*

* * *

# 21st February

But the tax collector stood at a distance. He would not even lift his eyes to heaven, but beat his breast. 'God have mercy on me, a sinner.'

Luke 18:13

*Your greatness, Lord, beggars all description;*
*And my littleness is beyond words.*
*You are holy; I am stained with many sins.*
*Ashamed, I dare not lift my eyes to meet Your sweet,*
*Familiar face, and yet if I do not adore You, I am not at peace.*
*So, with bowed head and folded hands, let me sing the story of Your greatness.*
*You will not turn away from the loving prayer of the lowliest of Your servants.*

*Tulsi Das (1543–1623) poet and translator in the Hindi language.*

Look up! Do not be afraid – He loves you . . . not the you

that you want to be, or the you that you ought to be, but He loves you just as you are.

* * *

# 22nd February

Remember your Creator in the days of your youth . . .

Ecclesiastes 12:1

I wonder how many thousands of women all over the world have memories of the Guide Movement? This day is the joint birthday of the founders of Scouting and Guiding, Lord and Lady Baden-Powell, and on this special day Guides 'think'. A Thinking Day is such a good idea – days get so full that we just don't get to thinking of wider horizons than walking the dog in the park, moaning in the store because they do not immediately stock what we want, or buying new shoes for the children.

Lord, may I remember today that youth is not the only time to think of You – from my routine chores lift my mind to think of all the worthwhile things that Guides do so may I encourage all those with initiative, personality and skill to lead young lives, wherever they are in the world . . . You created us all.

*Creator of life and light, we bless Thee for the beauty of the world, for sunshine and flowers, for clouds and stars, for the first radiance of dawn and the last glow of sunset. We thank Thee for physical joy, for the smell of rain on dry ground, for hills to climb and hard work to do, for music that lifts our hearts to heaven and for friendship. For all the beauty and the joy of home love, for mother love, for child love, for the joy of the sense of Thy presence we thank Thee O Lord.*

*Guide Prayer*

* * *

# 23rd February

Jesus said: 'The time is coming when true worshippers will worship the Father in spirit and truth, for they are the kind of worshippers the Father seeks.'

John 4:23

Whom dost thou worship in this lonely dark corner of a temple with doors all shut? Open thine eyes and see thy God is not before thee! He is there where the tiller is tilling the hard ground and where the path-maker is breaking stones. He is with them in sun and in shower, and his garment is covered in dust. Put off thy holy mantle and even like Him come down on the dusty soil . . .

Come out of thy meditations and leave aside thy flowers and incense! What harm is there if thy clothes become tattered and stained? Meet Him and stand by Him in toil and in sweat of thy brow.

Rabindranath Tagore, Bengali poet

*Forgive me, Lord, that I feel more comfortable cocooned within my world, my family, my church, my needs . . . I forget that I meet Christ in darker moments, in unsavoury surroundings, in lives of those who need Him just as I need Him. Open my eyes today.*

* * *

# 24th February

Jesus said: 'But I tell you, love your enemies and pray for those who persecute you.'

Matthew 5:44

If you have a negative feeling – worry, fear, anxiety, depression, hate, resentment – and it does not go away when you meditate, you must take immediate action . . . *make* yourself act quickly upon the opposite of that state . . . It is easy enough to act kindly if you feel kindly . . . the moment you feel hate or fear or pride think of the opposite state and act quickly upon it. If you do this you will find that you overcome the feeling in a wonderful way and you will have more power over the next mood.

Adela Curtis

*God only knows the love of God –*
*O that it now were shed abroad*
*In this poor stony heart!*

*Charles Wesley*

* * *

# 25th February

After the death of Moses the servant of the Lord, the Lord said to Joshua, son of Nun, Moses' assistant: 'Moses my servant is dead. Now then, you and all these people, get ready to cross the Jordan River into the land I am about to give them – to the Israelites . . . As I was with Moses, so I will be with you: I will never leave you or forsake you.

Be strong and courageous because you will lead these people to inherit the land I swore to their forefathers to give them. Be strong and very courageous. Be careful to obey all the law my servant Moses gave you; do not turn from it to the right or to the left, that you may be successful wherever you go.

Do not let this Book of the Law depart from your mouth, meditate on it day and night, so that you may be careful to do everything written in it . . . Be strong and courageous. Do not be terrified; do not be discouraged, for the Lord your god will be with you wherever you go.'

Joshua 1:1–9

* * *

# 26th February

For this reason I kneel before the Father . . . I pray that out of His glorious riches He may strengthen you with power through His Spirit in your inner being.

Ephesians 3:14–16

I think that the church, the lovely body of believers, could really minister to each member in prayer for each others' secular employment. Do you know the secular employment of all the members of your church? Does what they do in the day concern you? You may share your own spiritual needs but are you free enough to share your work problems? We are whole people, and if your work is God-given, a vocation, shouldn't it be of primary concern for us to pray for each other!

Elspeth Stephenson

*He bids us build each other up,*
*And, gathered into one,*
*To our high calling's glorious hope*
*We hand in hand go on.*

*Charles Wesley*

* * *

# 27th February

So Ahab went home, sullen and angry . . . he lay on his bed sulking and refused to eat.

1 Kings 21:4

It sounds as though King Ahab was reliving his 'terrible-twos'. Almost beyond belief that a king would behave in such a manner merely because he could not immediately have his own way . . . yet another story of greed, deceit and violence, and the influence of a strong woman. The compelling stories from the Old Testament are so believable because of the very fact that we know that base human nature is exactly the same today when untouched by the saving love of Christ Jesus. Lord, You know how many times I could act badly, think thoughts that I would never want anyone to share. You know these things yet You still offer me Your love – I shall never understand.

*Lord, make us strong, for You alone know*
*How oft we turn our faces from the foe:*
*How oft when claimed by dark temptations hour*
*We lose our hold on You and of Your power.*

*W.V. Jenkins*

* * *

# 28th February

Your fasting ends in quarrelling and strife . . . you cannot fast as you do today and expect your voice to be heard on high.

Isaiah 58:4

What a sorry picture Isaiah was painting – more of a farce than a fast. And as the centuries roll by human nature doesn't change one iota . . . we continue our pretence of self-denial . . . Lent gives us the excuse to feel righteous but we never truly get to grips with fasting. Many nutritionists claims that a one-day-a-week fast or month-long fast is beneficial for body and mind, but we spurn fasting as akin to becoming anorexic. Lord, how I wish I could fast from the clamour of the television – the demands on frayed nerves – as well as the temptations from the fridge. I want to feel well both in mind and body and to be fit and ready to worship.

*Far better to be a bit overweight but at peace and radiating the love of Christ, than to be model-thin and totally self-preoccupied and obsessed.*

*Sheila Walsh*

* * *

# 1st March

We love because He first loved us. If anyone says, 'I love God' yet hates his brother, he is a liar.

1 John 4:19

Hilary Anderson was a member of the Methodist Youth

Exchange team which visited Hong Kong and Korea in 1987. She stayed with a Mr and Mrs Ko in a traditional Korean home in Seoul, and went each morning with Mrs Ko to the 5 a.m. prayer meeting. On the first morning, they returned from the prayer meeting as dawn was breaking, walking through the streets hand in hand. Mrs Ko, using her expressive face and halting English, turned to Hilary and said: 'God love is . . . we . . . God . . . love. Because we . . . God . . . love . . . we connect!' They were words spoken from the heart which broke through all barriers of culture, language and age. She spoke the international and eternal truth of God's love.

*Let there be love shared among us,*
*Let there be love in our eyes,*
*May now your love sweep this nation*
*Cause us O Lord to arise.*
*Give us a fresh understanding of brotherly love that is real,*
*Let there be love shared among us – let there be love.*

*D. Bilbrough*

* * *

# 2nd March

I am making a way in the desert and streams in the wasteland.

Isaiah 43:19

The Women's World Day of Prayer is one of the most stimulating and uplifting experiences. I join with sisters at the store check-out, queue with them in doctor's waiting room or hospital, and stand shoulder to shoulder waiting for a bus – yet it is a rare jewel of an occasion to pray together. Lord, thank You for the special sharing sisterhood of this international and interdenominational day – thank You that I can come to this oasis in the desert of denominational barriers and throughout Your world we women, bring You our own, heartfelt praise.

*It's great outpouring of praise, intercession, celebration, penitence and thanksgiving has helped to irrigate the desert places of the world's life – and been a stimulus to Christian caring and compassion everywhere.*
*Dr John Newton on Womens' World Day of Prayer.*

* * *

# 3rd March

Another of His disciples, Andrew, Simon Peter's brother, spoke up, 'here is a boy with five small barley loaves and two small fish.'

John 6:8–9

So much has been written and spoken on the miracle Jesus performed with the five small loaves and two small fish, but today I just want to home in to a fact that seems to have gone unheeded. No little lad would have turned up to hear the great Teacher with a neat picnic that he had packed himself . . . oh no! He arrived breathless and eager, clutching the food his mother had packed for him. In that simple act I see a continuing miracle of the 'chain reaction of care'. And without that unknown mother, one of the greatest stories from the gospels would not have happened. Lord, steer me into the chain links of service, help me to do my small part, unnoticed, unnamed but whatever I do may it be for Jesus' sake.

*O Bread of Life, Thou in Thy word hast said:*
*'Who feeds in faith on me shall never die'.*
*In mercy hear Thy hungry children's cry*
*'Father, give us this day our daily bread'.*

*W. H. Gill*

# 4th March

Then Jesus was led by the Spirit into the desert to be tempted by the devil. After fasting forty days and forty night, He was hungry. The tempter came to Him and said, 'If you are the Son of God, tell these stones to become bread.'

Jesus answered, 'It is written: "Man does not live by bread alone, but on every word that comes from the mouth of God." '

Then the devil took Him to the holy city and made Him stand on the highest point of the temple. 'If you are the Son of God,' he said, 'throw yourself down. . . .'

Jesus answered him, 'It is also written: "Do not put the Lord your God to the test".'

Again the devil took Him to a very high mountain and showed Him all the kingdoms of the world and their splendour. 'All this I will give you,' he said, 'if you will bow down and worship me.'

Jesus said to him, 'Away from me, satan! For it is written: "Worship the Lord your God, and serve Him only".'

Matthew 4:1–10

* * *

# 5th March

But the wisdom that comes from heaven is first of all pure; then peace-loving, considerate, full of mercy . . .

James 3:17

Lent seems a God-given time of appraisal. A time to think. Then the space to incorporate into our daily living the product of our deeper thoughts. Oh, I don't like looking too deeply inside my heart – it's uncomfortable Lord, for You and I both know what a jaded mess I have become in spite of all the best of intentions. . . . I need to find You all over again – to rid my life of all that taints it and to live in Your wisdom, Your mercy . . . Help me, Lord.

*Give us, O Lord, a steadfast heart, which no unworthy thought can drag downwards; an unconquered heart, which no tribulation can wear out; an upright heart, which no unworthy purpose can tempt aside. Grant us also understanding to know You, diligence to seek You, wisdom to find You and a faithfulness finally to embrace You.*

*Thomas Aquinas*

* * *

# 6th March

> When the people heard this they were cut to the heart and said to Peter and the other apostles, 'What shall we do?'
>
> Acts 2:37

Indeed, this is a familiar cry: What shall we do? It is the cry we utter when we are at our most spiritually feeble and look to someone else to pick us up, dust us down, bathe the wounds and set us on our way again. Dr Martyn Lloyd-Jones once said that he thought Christianity was far too often presented as a remedy for all our problems – 'Come to the clinic and we'll give you all the loving care and attention that you need to help you with your problems.' But he says, 'In the Bible I find a barracks not a hospital. It is not a doctor you need but a drill sergeant. Here we are on the parade ground slouching around: a doctor won't help us. It is discipline we need!'

*Lord, I don't like discipline – not for me anyway – but deep down in my heart I know that is what I need. And I read too that You will discipline in love. . . . 'God disciplines us for our good, that we may share in His holiness.'*

*Hebrews 12:10*

* * *

# 7th March

> Jesus withdrew about a stone's throw beyond them, knelt down and prayed. 'Father if you are willing, take this cup from me, yet not my will but Yours be done.'
>
> Luke 22:44

A lift operator in one of the huge American hospitals had watched a mother and her little boy; first as out-patients, then he had chatted with them when the boy became a patient. The boy was very sick and the day came for his major operation. The mother came to the lift agitated and tense. Once inside the lift, the lift operator suggested they had a prayer before he operated the lift . . . his prayer was short and to the point, but just what she needed. 'Dear Lord, we pray for little Billie, we know he is in Your hands. And right now we pray for his Mom, 'cos she kinda needs you real bad too.'

*O Love Divine, that stooped to share*
*Our sharpest pang, our bitterest tear,*
*On Thee we cast each earth-born care –*
*Living and dying, Thou art near.*

*Oliver Wendell Holmes*

* * *

# 8th March

Create in me a pure heart, O God, and renew a steadfast spirit within me . . .

Psalm 51:10

*Jesus, come to me now that I need You,*
*Bring Your goodness in, cleanse my heart anew.*
*Take away my doubt, take away my fear,*
*Cause my heart to know that You're ever near.*
*Simply now I cry; 'Lay Your hand on me'*
*Meet, O Master dear, every need in me.*
*Lord, I reach to You though my faith is small,*
*Trusting that Your love knows no bounds at all.*

*David Barcham*

Lord, I admit my need . . . a need for Your strength and love every hour of every day . . . come and bless me, reach out and touch me with Your nail-imprinted hands . . . I open my life to You.

* * *

## 9th March

Hear O Israel, The Lord our God is One. Love the Lord your God with all your heart and with all your soul and with all your strength.

Deuteronomy 6:5

Those of us who are healthy co-ordinate our minds and bodies in spontaneous reflex – we don't need to stop and think about it. But anyone who has watched the struggles of a stroke victim or accident victim on the long haul to rehabilitate knows that mind and body are so separate that enormous effort is necessary to blend them into harmony again. Old-timers would not be embarrassed to ask in the street 'How is your soul?' . . . again recognition that the soul too is separate from our body and mind. Lord, I roar through the day, burning out my body, my mind in seven different directions. . . . I've almost mislaid my soul with neglect. Help me refocus on my 'whole' self. . . . redirect my love, my life and my worship.

*All I have I offer*
*All I hope to be –*
*Body, soul and spirit,*
*All I yield to Thee.*

*Godfrey Thring (adapted)*

* * *

## 10th March

I will lift up my eyes to the hills – where does my help come from? My help comes from the Lord. . . .

Psalm 121:1

The versatile entertainer Roy Castle revealed how God had saved his marriage. 'Our marriage had become very tense and we had started "biting" each other. It was the pressure of life, not just showbiz, which did it. It happens in many families, the man does a job and the wife has to do all the housework and bring up the children, and the pressures build. It even got to the point that Fiona got down on her knees and prayed for God to help her.' A friend became increasingly worried about Fiona's unhappiness and she phoned her. Roy says of that phone call: 'Thankfully our marriage was saved by the phone call – it was almost a hotline to God!'

*How pleased and blest was I*
*To hear the people cry,*
*Come! let us seek our God today!*

*Isaac Watts*

* * *

# 11th March

The entire law is summed up in a single command: 'Love your neighbour as yourself.' If you keep on biting and devouring each other, watch out or you will be destroyed by each other.

So, I say live by the Spirit, and you will not gratify the desires of the sinful nature. For the sinful nature desires what is contrary to the Spirit, and the Spirit what is contrary to the sinful nature. . . .

The acts of the sinful nature are obvious: sexual immorality, impurity and debauchery, idolatry and witchcraft; hatred, discord, jealousy, fits of rage, selfish ambition, dissensions, factions and envy: drunkenness, orgies and the like.

I warn you, as I did before, that those who live like this will not inherit the kingdom of God.

Galations 5:14–22

* * *

# 12th March

For God so loved the world that He gave His one and only Son that whosoever believes in Him shall not perish but have eternal life.

John 3:16

*For God – the Lord of Earth and Heaven,*
*So loved – and longed to see forgiven,*
*The World – in sin and pleasure mad,*
*That He gave – the greatest gift he had:*
*His only Son – to take our place,*
*That whosoever – o what grace,*
*Believeth – placing simple trust,*
*In Him – the Righteous and the Just,*
*Should not perish – shall not be lost in sin,*
*But have Eternal Life – in Him.*

*Anon*

Love so amazing so divine demands my soul, my life, my all.

Isaac Watts

* * *

# 13th March

'Quick, get up!' he (the Angel) said, and the chains fell off Peter's wrists.

Acts 12:7

To lose our chains we need to know that God is in charge. Nothing is ever gained by reeling and losing heart, or becoming bowed down by melancholy reflections. St Paul wrote that every believer ought to be fervent in spirit, as James Moffatt translated those words: 'maintain a spiritual glow'. The great difficulty for some of us is to get and then maintain the glow. We keep the chains too tightly . . . we grow weary with the frustrating and unanswered conditions of life. Even our favourite Bible passages, or cheerful hymns, fails to lift up our hearts. The psalmist was aware of the chains which held him (Psalm 31); perhaps the biggest realisation was that the everlasting Lord had known him perfectly all the time, when his chains were the tightest.

W. H. Bourne.

*Blessings abound where'er He reigns;*
*The prisoner leaps to lose his chains:*

*Isaac Watts*

* * *

# 14th March

Jesus went into Galilee, proclaiming the good news of God. 'The time has come,' he said . . . 'Repent and believe the good news!'

Mark 1:15

Repentance is not an overnight transformation which we bring about ourselves. It is not a case of 'Today I'm short-tempered, over-indulgent and self-centred but tomorrow I'll repent and it will all have gone.' That's not what it is like. True conversion and repentance is very simply and humbly turning back to God and saying, 'I'm short-tempered, over-indulgent and self-centred: can You help?'

Delia Smith

*When the people heard this, they were cut to the heart and said to Peter and the other apostles: 'Brothers, what shall we do?'*

*Peter replied: 'Repent and be baptised, every one of you, in the name of Jesus Christ so that your sins may be forgiven.'*

*Acts 2:28*

* * *

# 15th March

For I am the Lord your God who takes hold of your right hand and says to you, 'Do not fear, I will help you.'

Isaiah 41:13

A little child automatically puts up its hand to the parent when about to cross a road, but 'growing-up' involves independence; soon, too soon, the child doesn't want to hold hands. The parallel with our attitude to God is only too painfully obvious. Yet God has always wanted to take our hand . . . forgive me Lord, that I have been too big to admit my need, too proud to acknowledge my longing for Your help. . . . Today, in quiet and simple meditation, I give you back the hand I tore away . . . hold me, help me, love me. . . .

*When I turn to the Scriptures . . . I see it enough to acknowledge one's nothingness and surrender oneself like a child into God's arms.*

*St Therese of Lisieux*
*who died aged 24*

* * *

# 16th March

This is the message we have heard from Him and declare to you; God is Light; in Him there is no darkness at all.

1 John 1:5

*The Light of God surrounds me.*
*The Love of God enfolds me.*
*The power of God protects me.*
*The Presence of God watches over me.*
*Wherever I am, God is.*

*Anon*

The most helpful way to use the prayer above is to say each line and pause before going on to the next line. Perhaps repeat each line with gentle pauses – breathe slowly, be still, feel the peace of God flooding your soul with Light, Love, Power, His Presence . . . now.

* * *

# 17th March

Jesus said: 'Be careful, or your hearts will be weighed down with dissipation, drunkeness and the anxieties of life, and that day (the Kingdom of God) will close on you unexpectedly. . . .'

Luke 21:34

Our Lord Jesus was at pains to stress the fact that the

Kingdom of God would take everyone by surprise. His entreaties were to be watchful, to be careful, to be on the alert . . . no one would know the day. We are not very good at following His advice – it often appears that we have forgotten the Kingdom will come at all, the way we are so preoccupied with 'the anxieties of life'. To our shame we are even surprised when mini miracles occur – Forgive me Lord, that I only look to Your power in the past – I don't seem to register Your power for the present moment . . . the here and now for me.

*If the Lord wants to surprise His people, He has only at once to give them an answer. No sooner do they receive an answer than they say, 'Who would have thought it?'*

*C. H. Spurgeon*

* * *

# 18th March

*God is our refuge and strength,*
*an ever present help in trouble.*
*Therefore we will not fear, though the earth give way*
*and the mountains fall into the heart of the sea,*
*though its waters roar and foam and the mountains*
*quake with their surging . . .*
*Nations are in uproar,*
*kingdoms fall;*
*Come and see the works of the Lord -*
*He makes wars cease to the ends of the earth,*
*He breaks the bow and shatters the spear. . . .*
*Be still, and know that I am God;*
*I will be exalted among the nations*
*I will be exalted in the earth.*
*The Lord Almighty is with us.*

*Psalm 46*

* * *

# 19th March

'Martha, Martha,' the Lord answered, 'you are worried and upset about many things, but only one thing is needed.'

Luke 10:41

O Lord, I feel so much like Martha today! I worry over the family, over the housekeeping and over bigger bills – I get upset when there's a difference of opinion and hasty words. . . .

I get upset when I see loved ones getting old and frail, and I can't seem to help. . . . Give me Your quiet, Your strength so that I can stand back from all the niggles and tensions of the day. Lord, I want to see Jesus – to serve Jesus – to make Him the centre of my life. It is the one thing I need to do yet the fear of such commitment leaves me dithering and making excuses to avoid that very thing; that one act of worship and dedication. I'm asking for Your help . . . take me, use me and overflow my life with joy.

*Forth in Thy name, O Lord, I go*
*My daily labour to pursue:*
*Thee, only Thee, resolved to know*
*In all I think or speak, or do.*

*Charles Wesley*

* * *

# 20th March

Jesus said: 'When you fast, do not look sombre as the hypocrites do, for they disfigure their faces to show men that they are fasting.

Matthew 6:16

Evidently in the early writings, the word for hypocrite was the same as the word for actor, and in this vivid sentence Jesus gave a sketch we all understand. We all know people who make a meal of things – who go overboard to let everyone know just how wonderful they are! In this holy season of Lent, I pray for honesty – I am not wonderful, I am not what other people think of me – I am self-centred, quick-tempered and so very much like the people Jesus branded as hypocrites. Lord, I want to fall at Your feet, and through the tears of my confession cleanse me, build me, create in me a new heart and attitude: away with self . . . and bring me to humble self-sacrifice.

*Alone in the wilderness my Lord fasted:*
*Alone, tempted yet He remained true –*
*Alone in my wilderness, Lord Jesus Christ*
*Keep me loving and worshipping You.*

* * *

# 21st March

Because He himself suffered when He was tempted, He is able to help those who are being tempted.

Hebrews 2:18

It seems almost a law of life, dear Lord, that after every great moment I experience I swing from the stars to the mud. And it is while I am struggling in the mud of my own defeat that Satan comes to me as the accuser using my weariness and discouragement, my moods and my depressions to cause me to doubt You. Teach me to resist the devil, Lord, just as You did. Cause me to be vigilant, conscious that he is ever ready to trip me up. May I, like You, triumph over him by submitting to the Father's will.

Joyce Huggett

*When I'm tempted to do wrong –*
*Make me steadfast, wise and strong. . . .*
*When I fall (or rather run into temptation)*
*Father take my hand – pick me up, turn me round*
*And fix my eyes on Jesus my Lord.*

* * *

# 22nd March

'We have only five loaves of bread and two fish,' the disciples answered. Jesus said: 'Bring them here to me!'

Matthew 14:17–18

We have only – we often use the word only in a disparaging way. Sometimes it's used as an excuse . . . we couldn't do so and so because we only . . . Lord, how often have I wailed and been negative in my thinking. I want to learn the humility to turn things over to You – to bring whatever I have and however I feel to my Lord that You will mould me and use me for Your glory. In these quiet moments I kneel in dedication of this day and of myself – I bring myself and may the warmth of Your acceptance be my benediction.

*To Thee we come; refresh Thou us*
*With food from Thy most holy board,*
*Until the kingdoms of this world*
*Become the kingdom of the Lord.*

*M. F. C. Willson*

* * *

# 23rd March

Can the Ethiopian change his skin or the leopard his spots?

Jeremiah 13:23

This attitude has lingered – on the one hand we claim that Jesus can change the lives of the worst person on earth whilst still, deep down, we doubt people can really be changed . . . can the leopard change his spots? Lord, I'm prejudiced . . . I make judgements on people . . . and I think I am so right. Lord, I cannot change myself but I put all my trust in You that You can change me – change me from arrogance to sympathy, from complacency to a searching, eager faith.

*When disillusion chains our feet*
*And might and money turn to dust,*
*When exile, desert or defeat*
*Have left us nothing else to trust:*
*And last our spirit understands*
*The strength of peaceful, nail-scarred hands.*

*A drifting nation in decline*
*Can turn to just and loving ways . . .*
*And people empty, bruised, ashamed,*
*Can find rebirth to joy and praise –*
*and churches, wakened, can*
*exchange a huddled death for power to change.*

*Brian Wren*

* * *

# 24th March

One evening David got up from his bed and walked around on the roof of his palace. From the roof he saw a woman bathing. The woman was very beautiful . . .

2 Samuel 11:2–3

David – the mighty King David, God's annointed leader, the writer of psalms rich in devotion to God and psalms of abject misery and repentance – this same David saw a beautiful woman and wanted her. When you read the full story you will follow how the walk along the roof, the apparently innocent voyeurism, led to deceit, adultery and murder. Other people's downfall is so easily traced – we are not so concerned with our own temptations. Lord, I need to take care . . . I need to be strong . . . to be true . . . save me in my weakness, Lord. Things that look beautiful are not necessarily right.

*The tempter is also capable of using our innermost thoughts and desires to bring about our downfall. He launches his attack against our mind, our will and our passions so that even though we know that a certain course of action is not permissible for the Christian, we do it; even though we know that a certain place is riddled with temptation, we go there. And Satan wins another battle. . . .*

*Joyce Huggett*

* * *

# 25th March

He was despised and rejected by men,
a man of sorrows, and familiar with suffering.
Like one from whom men hide their faces he was despised
and we esteemed him not.
Surely, he took up our infirmities and carried our sorrows,
yet we considered him stricken by God,
smitten by him and afflicted.
But he was pierced for our transgressions,
he was crushed for our iniquities;
the punishment that brought us peace was upon him,
and by his wounds we are healed.
We all, like sheep, have gone astray,
each of us has turned to his own way;
and the Lord has laid on him the iniquity of us all.

Isaiah 53:2–7

* * *

# 26th March

Whoever does not love does not know God because
God is Love.

1 John 4:8

All sorts of people are fond of repeating the Christian statement that 'God is Love'. But they don't seem to notice that the words 'God is Love' have no real meaning unless God contains at least two persons. Love is something that one person has for another person . . . they really mean 'Love is God.' Christians believe that the living, dynamic activity of love has been going on in God forever and has created everything else. And that is perhaps the most important difference between Christianity and all other religions – that in Christianity, God is not a static thing – but a dynamic pulsating activity, a life, almost a kind of drama . . . almost, if you won't think me irreverent, a kind of dance.

C. S. Lewis

*God is Good! We sing about it, God is good, we celebrate.*
*God is good, no more doubt about it, God is good, we know it's true.*
*And when I think of His love for me my heart fills with praise*
*And I feel like dancing –*

*Graham Kendrick*

* * *

# 27th March

I have set my rainbow in the clouds, and it will be the sign of my covenant between me and the earth.

Genesis 9:13

All heads turn at the sight of a rainbow, but what is it really? Merely plain drops of water shot through with sunlight, and from a different angle there is no visible rainbow at all. Is that why lives can appear so different? On one level a person seems quite ordinary until lit by the light of God's Son . . . then they become extra-ordinary . . . the love through them gives colour and vitality to their dealings with others. Lord, help me to see that we are all so very ordinary – but Your touch can make each one of us extra-ordinary.

*Sun of our life, Thy quickening ray,*
*Sheds on our path the glow of day. . . .*
*Our rainbow arch Thy mercy's sign*
*All, save the clouds of sin, are Thine.*

*Oliver W. Holmes*

* * *

# 28th March

When Elizabeth heard Mary's greeting, the baby leaped in her womb, and Elizabeth was filled with the Holy Spirit.

Luke 1:41

The biblical meaning of 'filled' means more literally 'controlled'. Filled with rage was being so angry that the person was completely taken over, consumed, controlled by that rage. When we think of a person being filled with bitterness their faces show that their lives are controlled by that cancerous emotion. Lord, I pray today that Your Holy Spirit might fill my life, that I might be controlled by goodness and gentleness until there is no place for anger or bitterness or anything else which spoils and debases life. I am praying . . . so hard . . . so very hard.

*Fill Thou my life, O Lord my God*
*In every part with praise;*
*That my whole being may proclaim*
*Thy being and Thy ways.*

*Hortius Bonar*

* * *

# 29th March

So then, those who suffer according to God's will should commit themselves to their faithful Creator and continue to do good.

1 Peter 4:19

Anne Steele's family owned a timber business, and as faithful Baptists were well respected. Anne was fully launched on plans for her marriage and she was very much in love. Sadly, before the wedding her fiance drowned in an accident. For a while it seemed as though her whole life had been ruined. But Anne held to her strong faith, she committed the rest of her life to her Creator and wrote some spiritual and helpful poetry – she never knew the love of a family of her own but she was adored by all who knew her. Lord, when things don't go according to my plan give me strength to remain faithful.

*Divine Instructor, gracious Lord,*
*Be Thou for ever near:*
*Teach me to love Thy sacred word,*
*And view my Saviour there.*

*Anne Steele*

* * *

# 30th March

Strengthen the feeble hands, steady the knees that give way, say to those with fearful hearts, 'Be strong, do not fear'.

Psalm 35:3

We only have to read the 'problem pages' in magazines to realise what a lot of worried people there are around us. Worries great and small – over health, relationships, money, children, jobs and unemployment . . . people desperate for advice, comfort and direction. They turn to anyone and anywhere, except to God. Lord, when I am churned up inside, worried, fearful and trembling, remind me of the great thread of encouragement in Your holy word, whether from prophet, psalmists, apostle, visionary or Jesus Himself – 'Be strong, do not fear . . . I am with you always. . . .' I turn to You, Lord on my knees, I turn for strength.

*I have been driven many times to my knees by the overwhelming conviction that I had nowhere else to go.*

*Abraham Lincoln*

* * *

# 31st March

Jesus answered Pilate: 'You are right in saying I am a king. In fact for this reason I was born . . . to testify to the truth.'
'What is truth?' asked Pilate.

John 18:38

Pilate was caught in a political situation – no wonder he had to ask, 'What is truth?' Too often political manoeuvring distorts the truth; people have been known to be economical with the truth as well. Pilate wanted to wriggle out of all responsibility for Jesus – faced with The Truth, he turned his back, washed his hands and moved Jesus conveniently out of his life. But Jesus cannot be set aside so easily: there comes a time for all of us when we have to face up to truth – shrug and wriggle, pour out excuses as we will, that truth will stand forever. . . . Jesus came into the world to testify to, and confront us with His Truth.

*To the Jews who had believed Him, Jesus said, 'If you hold to my teaching, you are really my disciples. Then you will know the truth and the truth will set you free.'*

*John 8:31–32*

* * *

# 1st April

David asked, 'Is there anyone still left of the house of Saul to whom I can show kindness for Jonathan's sake?' Now, there was a servant of Saul's household named Ziba. . . . Ziba answered the King, 'There is still a son of Jonathan; he is crippled in both feet.'
'Where is he?' the King asked.
Ziba answered, 'He is at the house of Makir son of Ammiel in Lo Debar.'
So Kind David had him brought from Lo Debar, from the house of Makir son of Ammiel.
When Mephibosheth son of Jonathan, the son

of Saul, came to David, he bowed down to pay him honour.

David said, 'Mephibosheth!'

'Your servant,' he replied.

'Don't be afraid,' David said to him, 'for I will surely show you kindness for the sake of your father Jonathan. I will restore to you all the land that belonged to your grandfather Saul, and you will always eat at my table.'

2 Samuel 9:1–8

* * *

# 2nd April

Near the cross of Jesus stood His mother, His mother's sister, Mary the wife of Clopas, and Mary of Magdala.

John 19:25

The vigil at the bedside of someone who is terminally ill, or the daily pain of living with a handicapped child or senile relative – these can all be described as 'foot of the cross experiences'. As those women stood around the cross of Jesus in their aching distress they were totally impotent to help. Nothing they could do or say was any good – they must have felt half mad with anguish and frustration. But they didn't run away – they stayed with Jesus to the bitter end because they loved Him so much. And it is love today which holds men and women in their 'foot of the cross experiences'. They can do nothing but love – and go on loving, and go on just being with their loved one. Jesus stands with them.

*Near the cross I'll watch and wait –*
*Hoping, trusting ever*

*Frances Jane van Alstyne*

* * *

# 3rd April

Carrying His own cross, He went out to The Place of the Skull. . . . Here they crucified Him.

John 19:17

And my thoughts went to those dear Negro folk of the South in the days of their captivity, when they sang their songs of sorrow in a strange land. They were there, at the foot of the cross: they knew what cruel suffering meant. Out of that suffering, they had sung, 'Were you there when they crucified my Lord?' For He, the Crucified, was one with them, and they were one with Him. And we must be ready to go into the midst of strife, where His brethren – the poor, the oppressed, the afflicted – are still suffering. For He is still there, suffering with them in their midst; and in our love for them we show our love to Him.

C. F. Andrews

*Were you there when they nailed Him to the tree?*
*Sometimes it causes me to tremble, tremble, tremble:*
*Were you there when they nailed Him to the tree?*

*American Folk Hymn*
*Arranged by Frances Westbrook*

* * *

# 4th April

But one thing I do: forgetting what is behind and straining towards what is ahead, I press on towards the goal. . . .

Philippians 3:13–14

When a marriage partner walks out, all the attendant hurt and bitterness churns over and over and it's almost impossible to forget the series of events leading to the trauma. But guilt, resentment, anger all thrive in a devastated heart. Then, more than at any other time, we need prayerful help to make definite actions to forget and reach out to what lies ahead. A woman whose husband left her after 32 years of marriage volunteered to work in a nursing home. She went on to night classes and became an activities director in the home. After six years she was able to thank God for restoring the joy in her new life – she reached out and in the business of caring for others found forgetting possible.

*When we reach out to others, we find the path God has for us to take. Lord I pray today for anyone I know in this situation.*

* * *

# 5th April

> Return to the Lord your God and let this prayer be your offering to Him: Forgive all our sins and accept our prayer and we will praise You as we have promised.
>
> Hosea 14:2

All our sins? All *my* sins? Lord, do I really know the release of forgiven sin? I return in this another day to pray to You, knowing my life is filled with promises that have not been kept, good intentions that fizzled out of the window, aware that I have said, thought and done things of which I am truly ashamed. I return and ask forgiveness . . . hear the deep silent prayer of my heart. . . . I wait to feel Your answer in a surge of renewed confidence and hope for tomorrow.

*God says: Child,*
*Place the fabric of your life in the vat of my love:*
*Watch as I withdraw the stains of sin –*
*Know that my grace makes you pure within –*
*Rejoice, for in me you will never be rejected*
*But always accepted and uniquely loved.*

*Joyce Huggett*

* * *

# 6th April

Jacob said: 'My years have been few and difficult, and they do not equal the years of the pilgrimage of my fathers.'

Exodus 47:9

Lord, have mercy upon us:

We have talked often of being a pilgrim people, but have been unwilling to venture far from our own sheltered and privileged position. We have claimed concern for social justice and righteousness, but have failed to put our lives behind our words. Lord have mercy upon us, cleanse and renew us. May all who struggle to bring justice and peace find the strengthening of Your spirit and the support of a caring community.

Taken from Prayers for Asia Sunday

*No matter what you may do, the Lord said;*
*Each step is only a phase, the Lord said:*
*My love will strengthen you as you go along*
*For you're my travelling, wandering race,*
*You're the people of God.*

*Estelle White*

* * *

# 7th April

Give thanks to the Lord, for He is good. His love endures for ever.

Psalm 136:1

With so many twists and turns in life we come face to face with occasions when giving thanks seems impossible. When marriages split up – relatives appear in court – husbands are in danger through the job and placement in the world – give thanks? How? For me it is only in looking back that I realise how good the Lord has been and in the light of what He has already done, if I can't actually give thanks,

I can trust Him for today and the tomorrows of my life. Only He is good and only He will love me and sustain me for ever.

*Great is Thy faithfulness O God my Father*
*There is no shadow of turning with Thee:*
*Thou changest not, thy compassions, they fail not*
*As Thou hast been Thou for ever wilt be . . .*
*All I have needed Thy hand has provided*
*Great is Thy faithfulness, Lord unto me.*

*Thomas O. Chisholm*

* * *

# 8th April

They brought the colt to Jesus, threw their cloaks on the colt and put Jesus on it. As He went along people spread their cloaks on the road.

When He came near the place where the road goes down the Mount of Olives, the whole crowd of disciples began joyfully to praise God in loud voices for all the miracles they had seen.

'Blessed is the king who comes in the name of the Lord! Peace in heaven and glory in the highest!'

Some of the Pharisees in the crowd said to Jesus: 'Teacher, rebuke your disciples!'

'I tell you,' Jesus replied, 'If they keep quiet the stones will cry out!'

As He approached Jerusalem and saw the city, He wept over it and said, 'If you, even you, had only known on this day what would bring you peace – but now it is hidden from your eyes . . . you did not recognise the time of God's coming to you.'

Luke 19:35–43 & 48

* * *

# 9th April

Let us then approach the throne of grace with confidence, so that we may receive mercy and find grace to help us in our time of need.

Hebrews 4:16

Whenever I hear the siren of an ambulance my heart goes out to the unknown person or persons in need. At those times how we long to know that help is on the way. It's all very different when we read in the Bible, Jesus saying to us that He came into the world to seek and to save the lost . . . but I do believe that the family of believers ought to be more aware of the needs of our friends and neighbours. We must not wait for the church to act as an ambulance – emergency only – we need to be in the midst of our community, seeing, listening, caring and encouraging with the grace of our Lord Jesus Christ given to us that we may give to others.

*In loving kindness Jesus came*
*My soul in mercy to reclaim,*
*And from the depths of sin and shame*
*Through grace He lifted me . . .*

*C. H. Gabriel*

* * *

# 10th April

The Lord is my shepherd, I shall lack nothing. He makes me lie down in green pastures . . .

Psalm 23:1–2

The author of one of the best-loved hymns of all time, died in the spring of 1910. Anna Laetitia Waring was 27 when her hymn 'In Heavenly Love Abiding' was published in her *Hymns and Meditations* which was so popular that it ran to ten editions. However, she was not just a writer of moving poems, but a doer of loving deeds. She took an active part in the Discharged Prisoners' Aid Society and was herself a prison visitor. She made her visits in an age when that kind of outreach had few supporters – especially amongst women. Anna lived all her life by the standards of the Gospel. To the prisoners who had despaired of kindness and a second chance, she brought the good news – a Saviour, their Saviour.

*Green pastures are before me*
*Which yet I have not seen;*
*Bright skies will soon be o'er me*
*Where the dark clouds have been:*

*Anna Laetitia Waring*

* * *

# 11th April

Those who passed by hurled insults at Him. . . . 'Come down from the cross if you are the Son of God!'

Matthew 27:39

How easy it is to jump on the bandwagon of mob abuse when the victim is unable to retaliate. So hurtful to the victim and also their family. We can see in our mind's eye the agonised body of Jesus hanging from the cross – a spectacle, the butt of offensive jibes. His mother watches, hearing the taunts, longing to see her son perform just one more miracle. It is a harrowing scene of blood, tears and anguish. Lord, I don't understand how people could have hurled insults at the carpenter who had done so much good – how can they still hurl insults at the risen Saviour? I'm ashamed at the depths to which a human heart can sink.

*'There cannot be a God of love,' say men, 'because if there were and He looked upon this world, His heart would break.' The church points to the cross and says, 'His heart does break'.*

*William Temple*
*Archbishop of Canterbury 1942–45*

* * *

# 12th April

Then Peter remembered the word the Lord had spoken to him: 'Before the cock crows today, you will disown me three times.'

Luke 2:61

Oh, the pain of being betrayed – the realisation that a friend, your own friend, has let you down. I pray today for all the broken relationships whether they be between friends or within families or partners. Lord, I pray for Your healing touch to the raw wounds which so quickly will turn septic and poison the months and years ahead. We all make mistakes, Lord, we are so eager to open our mouths without any care for the consequences – so I beg for humility . . . for true penitence . . . for the ability to weep at my unworthiness . . . and the willingness to make a fresh start.

*Three times Peter disowned his Lord.*
*And that same Lord said I must forgive seventy times seven. . . .*
*The creation of hell takes no time at all:*
*But a lifetime is taken to reach heaven.*

* * *

# 13th April

The cords of the grave coiled around me, the snare of death confronted me. In my distress I called to the Lord: I cried to my God for help.

Psalm 18:5–6

The chief priests and teachers of the law and elders of the synagogue watched the troublemaker dying in agony . . . and they jeered and mocked. The ordinary people stood helpless. The women who had hung on His every word . . . Jairus whose daughter now ran about in play, the men who had been leper outcasts, blind beggars, those who had held such high, heart-stopping hopes of the Nazareth

Man . . . the sun ceased to shine . . . death overtook the Son of God.

*Jesus cried out in a loud voice: 'My God, my God, why have You forsaken me?' And when Jesus had cried out again in a loud voice, He gave up His spirit.*

*Matthew 27:46 & 50*

* * *

# 14th April

I die every day – I mean that, brothers. . . .

1 Corinthians 15:31

*It all began in such a tiny way*
*My friend praised another and*
*I felt a stab of jealousy down deep inside my being.*

*I became irritable and bad-tempered*
*I sulked and wallowed in self-pity;*
*My work suffered – my friends suffered. . . .*
*How the Tempter must have been satisfied!*

*I need Your forgiveness, Lord,*
*I need Your help.*
*Teach me that it is only as I die to self*
*That the seed of jealousy will find nowhere to root.*

*Peter Bolt*

Christ's death on the cross generated moral forces which will be in operation in eternity. If some souls should ever feel moved to turn away from God and centre upon 'self', one glance at the Redeemer's scars will be sufficient to order all things within to the perfect order of heaven.

Mrs Penn Lewis

* * *

# 15th April

*This joyful Eastertide*
*What need is there for grieving?*
*Cast all your cares aside*
*And be not unbelieving:*

*No work for Him is vain,*
*No faith in Him mistaken.*
*For Easter makes it plain*
*His kingdom is not shaken:*

*Then put your trust in Christ*
*In waking and in sleeping:*
*His grace on earth sufficed –*
*He'll never quit His keeping:*

*Come, share our Easter joy*
*That death could not imprison,*
*Nor any power destroy*
*Our Christ, who is ARISEN!*

*Rev. Fred Pratt Green*

* * *

# 16th April

What you sow does not come to life unless it dies.

1 Corinthians 15:37

*The Waking earth at Easter reminds us – it IS true*
*That nothing ever really dies that is not born anew.*
*So trust God's all-wise wisdom*
*And doubt the Father never,*
*For in God's heavenly kingdom there is nothing lost for ever.*
*And, though our sins are scarlet,*
*God is ready to forgive*
*If we believe with all our hearts Christ died that we might live.*

*Anon*

*Now the green blade rises from the buried grain,*
*Wheat that in the dark earth many days has lain;*
*Love lives again, that with the dead has been:*
*Love is come again, like wheat that springs up green.*

*J. M. C. Crum*

* * *

# 17th April

Very early in the morning, while it was dark, Jesus got up, left the house and went off to a solitary place, where He prayed.

Mark 1:35

*Almighty God*
*Who made the delicate field daisy and the limitless reaches of space,*
*Who made the babe to suck and the soul to search,*
*Thank You for being God AVAILABLE!*
*No, more even than available.*
*Thank You for seeking me first –*
*For searching along the agonising road to Golgotha*
*Then finding me*
*Blindly supplying nails for Your Son's hands.*
*And when I finally found You, Lord,*
*Your bleeding hand was reaching for mine.*

*Susan Lenzkes*

If Jesus, the Son of God, needed to get away to a solitary place to pray – then how much more do I need that quietness to be still . . . and to really know, deep down in my soul, to know that You are God.

* * *

# 18th April

Jesus explained: 'Others like seed grown on good soil, hear the word, accept it and produce a crop, 30, 60 or even 100 times what was sown.'

Mark 4:20

The whole idea of 'receiving' God's word is also associated with my total availability to it. The whole ground of my life needs to be reachable. In a good garden there are no spots still littered with stones. There are no odd corners cluttered and choked out with weeds. There are no beaten paths where nothing at all can grow. All the ground has to be tilled. All the soil must finally be fitted for fruitlessness. It will take time to do this. But it must be done. The Spirit of God is very persistent. The Good Gardener must have full management. Christ comes to take over every area made arable.

W. Phillip Keller

*Christ, the loving Gardener*
*Tends these blossoms small –*
*Loves the little lilies*
*As the cedars tall.*

*Ella Armitage*

* * *

# 19th April

Then Jesus told Thomas, 'Because you have seen me, you have believed: blessed are those who have not seen me and yet believe.'

John 20:29

It is a fact that men experience the presence of God. Into our lives come times when, all unexpectedly, He shadows over us, steals into the inner recesses of our souls, and lifts us up in a wonderful joy and peace. The curtains of heaven are raised, and we find ourselves in heavenly peace in Christ Jesus. Sometimes these moments of visitation come to us in strange surroundings – on lonely country roads, in a classroom, at the kitchen sink. At such times of direct experience of Presence, we know that God is utterly real. When we are gazing into the sun we need no argument, no proof that the sun is shining.

Thomas R. Kelly

*I know that my Redeemer lives*
*What joy the blest assurance gives!*
*He lives, He lives, who once was dead;*
*He lives, my everlasting Head.*

*Samuel Medley*

* * *

# 20th April

And with Thee is wisdom. . . . Send her forth from the holy heavens, so that she may labour at my side and I may learn what pleases Thee.

Wisdom of Solomon 9:10

Most kind Jesus, grant me your grace to be at my side and share my labours, and remain with me right to the end. . . . You are the true peace of the heart, its only rest . . . I rest in You, the highest, the everlasting Good, and even as I lie down, sleep comes, and with sleep tranquility.

Thomas a Kempis

*Lord of all eagerness, Lord of all faith,*
*Whose strong hands were skilled at the plane and the lathe,*
*Be there at our labours, and give us, we pray*
*Your strength in our hearts, Lord, at the noon of the day.*

*Jan Struther*

* * *

# 21st April

And whatever you do, whether in word or deed, do it all in the name of the Lord Jesus

Colossians 3:17

Not only was Eric Liddell the holder of an Olympic Gold Medal for the 400 metres in 1924, but he was to become a saintly missionary in China who died prematurely in a Japanese prisoner internment camp. He has lived on in people's hearts as an inspiring athlete and Christian. The

Rev Arnold Bryson gave a brief address at Eric's funeral when he said: 'What was the secret of his consecrated life and far-reaching influence? Absolute surrender to God's will as revealed in Jesus Christ. His was a God-controlled life and he followed his Master and Lord with a devotion which never flagged, and with an intensity of purpose that made men see both the reality and power of true religion.'

*Be still my soul: the Lord is on thy side!*
*first line of Eric Liddell's*
*favourite hymn: True Finlandia*

* * *

# 22nd April

The angel of the Lord came and sat down under the oak in Ophrah that belonged to Joash the Abiezrite, where his son Gideon was threshing wheat in a wine press to keep it from the Midianites. When the angel of the Lord appeared to Gideon, he said, 'The Lord is with you, mighty warrior.'

'But Sir,' Gideon replied, 'if the Lord is with us, why has all this happened to us? Where are all his wonders that our fathers told us about when they said, "Did not the Lord bring us up out of Egypt?" But now the Lord has abandoned us and put us into the hand of Midian.'

The Lord turned to him and said, 'Go in the strength you have and save Israel out of Midian's hand. Am I not sending you?'

'But Lord,' Gideon asked, 'how can I save Israel? My clan is the weakest and I am the least in my family.'

The Lord answered: 'I will be with you. . . .'

Judges 6:11–16

* * *

# 23rd April

Now Thomas, (called Didymus) one of the twelve,
was not with the disciples when Jesus came. . . .

John 20:24

I wonder why Thomas was missing for that momentous visit? Everyone else was huddled away behind the locked doors – in grief, in fear . . . where was Thomas? Perhaps he had been sent off to buy bread, he may even have gone home for a while. After a great deal of meditating on Thomas' whereabouts, I believe God had guided him out of the way for a specific purpose. I see that purpose as being for you and me, that as we read about Thomas, the practical, no-nonsense man, who thought his friends had gone mad, we identify our deepest misgivings. How can it all be true? But also, through Thomas, I see the awe and humility that needed no more reasons; he knew he had met his Lord.

*'My pierced side, O Thomas see;*
*Behold my hands, my feet,' said He;*
*'Not faithless but believing be.'*
*No longer Thomas then denied;*
*He saw the feet, the hands, the side;*
*'You are my Lord and God,' he cried.*

*Jean Tisseraud (d. 1494)*

* * *

# 24th April

Jesus said: 'But small is the gate and narrow the road that leads to life, and only a few find it.'

Matthew 7:14

Andrew and Pauline decided to explore a footpath to the cliffs. It had become more overgrown than they realised and half way through they wondered if it was worth battling on. Carry on they did, and suddenly they emerged from the nettles and brambles right out on the cliff with a panoramic view of the sun shining all along the coast. If you are battling on life's road, keep going today – Jesus forecast a difficult road, but also promised to be with each one of us as we travel the narrow way. Anne Bronte wrote the lines below on 24th April, 1848 – they were published after her early death at 29. Her road was austere and sad, but her faith shone like the sun along the shores of time.

*Believe not those who say*
*The upward path is smooth,*
*Lest you should stumble in the way*
*And faint before the truth.*

*Anne Brontë (1820–1849)*

* * *

# 25th April

Jesus said: 'Before long, the world will not see me any more, but you will see me.'

John 14:19

It is not enough for you and me to hear other people say that Jesus rose from the dead, and it is not enough even for you and me to read the Bible . . . we want to see for ourselves. Just hearing of it does not make a man a new creature, it is seeing for yourself that works the miracle. Do not ask me for the mechanics of it or the psychology of it. When it happens it is unmistakable, and unforgettable, and no man who knows it is ever the same again. This is what we need – a personal encounter. If you want this personal encounter, then here is the way of it written clearly in Scripture: read John 14 until you know it by heart. Fasten these words with steel hooks to your heart and mind.

Kenneth Mackenzie

*Lord, may we see Your hands and side –*
*Touch You and feel Your presence near.*

*Christopher Porteous*

* * *

# 26th April

Zacchaeus wanted to see Jesus, but being a short man he could not, because of the crowd.

Luke 19:3

Tom Thumb may have been cute – but actually being short is a nightmare for many. They are the object of ridicule by cruel school 'friends', and feel generally scorned for not being 'average'. Take heart if you are small: Dr Isaac Watts, the great hymn writer, was five feet tall, and Charlotte Brontë, a bright star of the 19th century novelists, was just four feet nine! Lord, help me to look beyond the physique into the personality – to understand that largeness of heart, God-given gifts and inspiration are nothing to do with size. Small is beautiful! You are beautiful because God made you and God loves you.

*What matter who should whisper blame,*
*Or who should scorn or slight if but your God approve.*

*Anne Brontë*

* * *

# 27th April

Then Jesus said: 'If anyone would come after me, he must deny himself and take up his cross and follow me.'

Matthew 16:24

Many kids today who become Christians have no church background. If our material is wishy-washy sentimentalism, their picture of Jesus will be painted in those shades. . . . The harsh reality is seldom painted. Taking up the cross daily and following Christ are difficult words to fit into pretty songs. . . . Unless we allow people to come to grips with the very heart of the Gospel, which was born through suffering, we have failed in our artistry.

Sheila Walsh

*Inscribed upon the Cross we see*
*In shining letters:*
*God is Love!*

*Thomas Kelly*

* * *

# 28th April

Jesus said: 'Whoever serves me must follow me: and where I am my servant also will be.'

John 12:26

*O Thou who art the Light of the minds that know Thee,*
*the Life of the souls that love Thee*
*and the strength of the wills that serve Thee,*
*help us so to know Thee that we may truly love Thee,*
*so to love Thee we may fully serve Thee*
*whom to serve is perfect freedom*
*through Jesus Christ our Lord.*

*Eighth century Gelasian Sacramentary*

Lord it makes me feel part of a wonderful company of Your followers when I read prayers that are so ancient – it encourages me that I am not alone, millions of people before me, millions right now all over the world, and millions of people in the future will seek to serve Jesus Christ with their whole lives.

* * *

# 29th April

Come, let us sing for joy to the Lord;
Let us shout aloud to the Rock of our salvation.
Let us come before Him with thanksgiving
And extol Him with music and song.
For the Lord is the Great God
The Great King above all gods.
In his hand are the depths of the earth
And the mountain peaks belong to Him.

The sea is His, for He made it,
And His hands formed the dry land.
Come, let us bow down in worship,
Let us kneel before the Lord our Maker,
For He is our God and we are the people of His pasture,
The flock under His care.
Today – if you hear His voice
Do not harden your hearts.

Psalm 95:1–8

* * *

# 30th April

Behold, I am coming soon! My reward is with me, and I will give to everyone according to what he has done.

Revelation 22:12

*All that I am, all that I do, all that I'll ever have*
*I offer now to you.*
*Take and sanctify these gifts for Your honour, Lord.*
*Knowing that I love and serve You*
*Is enough reward.*
*All that I am, all that I do, all that I'll ever have*
*I offer now to You.*

*All that I dream, all that I pray,*
*All that I'll ever make I give to You today.*
*Take and sanctify these gifts for Your honour, Lord.*
*Knowing that I love and serve You*
*Is enough reward.*
*All that I am, all that I do*
*All that I'll ever have*
*I offer now to You.*

*Sebastian Temple*

The man who plants and the man who waters have one purpose, and each will be rewarded according to his own labour.

1 Corinthians 3:8

* * *

# 1st May

Paul said: '. . . so keep up your courage . . . for I have faith in God.'

Acts 27:25

Having survived the 1960s and 1970s, I am now absolutely convinced that we are not able to live without an injection of something additional in our lives. Four years ago I couldn't have said that. I believe absolutely in God, and during the time I have been working on this film (Chariots of Fire) all of these beliefs happened to solidify. I sometimes wonder why at the time of life when I had enough clout to put on a film like that, should I suddenly find the book?

David Puttnam

*I am not skilled to understand what God has willed . . .*
*What God has planned . . .*
*I only know at His right hand stands one*
*Who is my Saviour.*

*Dora Greenwell*

* * *

# 2nd May

All flying insects that walk on all fours are to be detestable to you. There are, however, some winged creatures that walk on all fours that you may eat.

Leviticus 11:20

An insect landed one day on a canvas. It was old canvas. It was a very small insect. It had no idea that the few centimetres of dull colour beneath its feet was part of one of the most famous paintings of all time – The Last Supper. It flew off without noticing any more than the dull blotch. Lord, I feel pretty much like an insect . . . my small patch is dull and I can't see anything else. Show me that my feet are planted on the earth You created. Earth is part of the vast globe You created. I am Your creation. And in receiving the bread and the wine I am joined in the communion of saints on earth and in heaven. Not so dull after all!

*The earth is the Lord's*
*and everything in it –*
*the world and all who live in it.*

*Psalm 24:1*

* * *

# 3rd May

Jesus said: 'I tell you the truth, unless an ear of wheat falls to the ground and dies, it remains only a single seed. But if it dies it produces many seeds.'

John 12:24

These are the last words of Archbishop Romero a few minutes before he was assassinated:

'You have just heard in the Lord's Gospel that we must not love ourselves so much that we refrain from plunging into those risks history demands of us, and that those wanting to keep out of danger will lose their lives. On the other hand, those who surrender to the service of people through love of Christ will live like the grain of wheat that dies.'

*Lord, I pray for parts of the world where the poor and oppressed are struggling for justice and freedom. Thank You for the men and women of conviction who are prepared to face even death in their service of Your children, whose lives inspire and whose memories produce seeds of response all over the world.*

* * *

# 4th May

Comfort, comfort my people, says your God.

Isaiah 40:1

Often misunderstanding is created by the fact that the words of the Bible have been translated, and words in

English may not have the precise meaning in Greek or Hebrew. The Greek verb to comfort, as in Isaiah 40:1, is *parakalein* and combines the words of exhort and encourage. In this setting, the comfort was to enable the people to stand on their own feet again – to meet their circumstances unbowed and undefeated. That kind of comfort is needed today. Not the 'Oh, you'll be all right' type comfort, but the deeper strength of God's comfort – His presence, His embracing Spirit to give us encouragement to meet the day ahead.

*'People want to be comforted . . . they need consolation – really need it and do not merely long for it.'*

*Dr Dale*

* * *

# 5th May

With the Lord, a day is like a thousand years and a thousand years are like a day.

2 Peter 3:8

Father, what a week! Full of blessings and frustrations. Thank You for sustaining me in my low moments and for taking hold of me when I've been caught up in my own self-confidence. Without You, my week would have been much the poorer; as it was, we have been through thick and thin together. For that I am eternally grateful. Now I lay the coming week before You – make me ready to serve You and all people in the days to come. Help me now, Father, to rest in Your presence so that I can begin the new week at peace with You and the world.

Prayer from 'All Year Round' (slightly adapted)

*O God, our help in ages past*
*Our hope for the days, weeks, months and years to come.*

* * *

# 6th May

One night, Eli, whose eyes were becoming so weak that he could barely see, was lying down in his usual place. The lamp of God had not yet gone out, and Samuel was lying down in the temple of the Lord, where the ark of God was. Then the Lord called Samuel.

Samuel answered, 'Here I am.' And he ran to Eli and said, 'Here I am; you called me.'

But Eli said, 'I did not call; go back and lie down.'

Again the Lord called, 'Samuel!'.

Then Eli realised that the Lord was calling the boy.

So Eli told Samuel, 'Go and lie down, and if He calls you say, "Speak Lord for your servant is listening." '

So Samuel went and lay down in his place.

The Lord came and stood there, calling as at the other times, 'Samuel! Samuel!' Then Samuel said, 'Speak Lord, for your servant is listening.'

1 Samuel 3:2–10

* * *

# 7th May

These commandments that I give you today are to be upon your hearts. Impress them on your children. Talk about them when you sit at home . . .

Deuteronomy 6:6–7

I've heard it said that for many people, the biggest challenge to the Christian witness is being able to share their faith with their children! Not so for the Israelites. They were instructed to keep alive the memory of their deliverance, to learn the commandment given to them and to include the children . . . to actually talk about the Scriptures as a way of life. There is a difference in ramming 'religion' down our children's throats and making the path of peace, justice and right living the normal, accepted path to take. Lord, free me from embarrassment – Your word is challenging, interesting, and worth talking about.

*The sins that mar our homes forgive;*
*From all self-seeking set us free;*
*Parents and children, may we live*
*In glad obedience, Lord, to Thee*

*Hugh Martin*

* * *

# 8th May

Strengthened by that food, Elijah travelled for forty days and forty nights until he reached Horeb . . . there he went into a cave –

1 Kings 19:8

Unusual is the person who can sail through life and say they have never felt at breaking point. The pace of modern life has very little to do with it – and things that crush us today are virtually the same in any century or culture. Fear, physical and mental exhaustion, war, pain, illness, bereavement, shock, unhappiness – all these are human hell. No one is immune whether old Testament prophet or pop super-star. Lord, I feel guilty at the strains that pull me down. I feel I should be able to cope so much better than I am doing . . . sometimes I just want to crawl into a cave. Please, rescue me.

*Hiding in Thee . . . hiding in Thee*
*Thou blest Rock of Ages*
*I'm hiding in Thee.*

*William O. Cushing*

* * *

# 9th May

I am the Lord, who exercises kindness, justice and righteousness on earth, for in these I delight, declares the Lord.

Jeremiah 9:24

Be kind and merciful, let none ever come to you without coming away better and happier. Be the living expression of God's kindness, kindness in your smile, kindness in your warm greeting. In the slums of Calcutta we are the light of God's kindness to the poor. To children, to the poor, to all who suffer and are lonely, give always a happy smile. Give them not only your care but also your heart.

Mother Teresa

*Lord of all kindliness, Lord of all grace,*
*Your hands swift to welcome, your arms to embrace,*
*Be there at our homing, and give us, we pray*
*Your love in our hearts, Lord, at the eve of the day.*

*Jan Struther*

* * *

# 10th May

Give thanks to the Lord for He is good; His love endures for ever.

Psalm 118:1

*Daylight is dawning, dew on the field,*
*Birds swell our praises, for beauty revealed;*
*Warm of the sunshine, cool of the breeze,*
*Whispers of music, dancing of leaves:*
*Thanks for Your gifts Lord, Thanks for each day*
*Thanks for Your bounty blessing our way.*

*Wonderful Saviour, always our friend,*
*Hear us Your children, on You we depend;*
*Peace is Your gift Lord, peace is our need,*

*Peace for each colour, peace for each creed.*
*Come to our home Lord, come Lord and stay*
*Be our Companion every new day.*

*Edwin Jukes*

Lord, make my life full of thankfulness and praise. Every day brings me your love, your care and your presence with me. Thank you, Lord, for everything.

Mary Batchelor

* * *

# 11th May

Though You have made me see troubles, many and bitter, You will restore my life again; from the depths of the earth You will again bring me up.

Psalm 71:20

None of us is immune to the disease of the decade – STRESS. Dr Thomas Holmes, a recognised authority on the subject of stress, measures stress in terms of 'units of change'. For example, the death of a loved one measures 100 units, divorce 73 units, pregnancy 40 units, moving house 25 units – even Christmas 12 units! His conclusion is that no one can handle more than 300 units of stress in a twelve-month period without suffering physically or emotionally during the next two years. Lord, help me to see that my impossibilities are Your possibles – my weakness is Your strength, and open my eyes to Your encouragement in the Bible.

*Bibles that are falling apart belong to the people who don't!*

* * *

# 12th May

Therefore my dear friends – continue to work out your salvation with fear and trembling . . .

Philippians 2:12

The end of self-surrender is salvation. To surrender to God is not very flattering to the ego, and that is why many would try, by learned arguments, to skip around the necessity. However, if you try to skip around it, you will trip over your unsurrendered self into unhappiness. The law of self-surrender is the only law that brings you from the kingdom of self into the Kingdom of God. . . . One of the greatest tragedies is that thousands will go to Church this coming Sunday, thinking that church attendance alone assures them a place in the kingdom of God.

Selwyn Hughes

*'Going to church doesn't make you a Christian any more than going to a garage makes you a motor car!'*

*Billy Graham*

* * *

# 13th May

. . . and Naomi was left without her two sons and her husband. . . . With her two daughters-in-law she left the place where she had been living and set out on the road that would take them back to the land of Judah.

Then Naomi said to her two daughters-in-law, 'Go back, each of you, to your mother's home. May the Lord show kindness to you as you have shown to your dead and to me. May the Lord grant that each of you will find rest in the home of another husband.' Then she kissed them and they wept aloud and said to her, 'We will go back with you to your people' . . . But Naomi said, 'Return home, my daughter's.'

At this they wept again. Then Orpah kissed her mother-in-law and said good-bye, but Ruth clung to her.

Ruth replied: 'Don't urge me to leave you . . . where you go I will go, and where you stay I will stay. Your people will be my people and your God my God.' When Naomi realised that Ruth was determined to go with her, she stopped urging her.

So the two women went on until they came to Bethlehem.

Ruth 1:5–19

* * *

# 14th May

Love does not delight in evil but rejoices with the truth. It always protects, always trusts, always hopes . . .

1 Corinthians 13:6–7

You will find, if you think for a moment, that the people who influence you are people who believe in you. In an atmosphere of suspicion, men shrivel up; but in the atmosphere of love they expand, and find encouragement and educative fellowship. Love 'thinketh no evil', imputes no motive, sees the bright side, puts the best construction on every action – to be trusted is to be saved. And if we try to influence or elevate others, we shall soon see that success is in proportion to their belief of our belief in them.

Henry Drummond

*Love is kind and suffers long*
*Love is meek and thinks no wrong*
*Love than death itself more strong;*
*Therefore give us love.*

*Christopher Wordsworth*

* * *

# 15th May

Be silent before the Sovereign Lord, for the day of the Lord is near.

Zephaniah 1:7

I'm just going to spend a few minutes relaxing – becoming aware of my Lord's presence with me.

I will be still. I listen to sounds around me, my breathing

becomes deeper, I focus on God, quietly expressing my love. I focus on my family, my friends, and pray for their renewal. I focus on me. I let go of my thoughts, I turn away from all words and actions that would preclude me from that right and full relationship with God my Saviour.

As I breathe in I imagine God's gentle Spirit filling me with all that is true and pure and lovely.

I breathe slowly – I am silent. . . .

*Be still and know that I am God . . . (repeat 3 times)*
*I am the Lord that healeth thee. . . . (repeat 3 times)*

*arr. Roland Fudge*

* * *

# 16th May

The trees of the Lord are well watered . . . there the birds make their nests. . . .

Psalm 104:17

I never fail to be amazed at the sight of a bird's nest. Its strength, for the tiny birds – its softness. The way grasses, twiglets and all sorts have been woven into shape; not by machine, but by a beak. Lord, I love the birds that sing on the morning air, they liven up the garden, the parks and the woods. There is something chirpy and happy about the presence of birds . . . their friendship lifts the heart. Thank you, Lord, for the birds which fly in and out of my day – they soar and swoop, come and go – but You Lord, are there all the time and the knowledge should give me more joy than the sight of the birds.

*He is with me everywhere,*
*And He knows my every care:*
*I'm as happy as a bird – and just as free*
*Jesus satisfies my soul.*

*H. Buffum*

* * *

# 17th May

From the rising of the sun to the place where it sets, the name of the Lord is to be praised.

Psalm 113:3

Lord Hailsham, the U.K's longest serving Lord Chancellor this century, was speaking on radio about the sudden death of his first wife Mary. She died following a riding accident and they had been married for 34 years. He said that his faith had not been shaken, but he just felt as though the sun didn't shine any more. Today, Lord, in the midst of bright early summer, surrounded by beauty and fresh growth, I pray for those who have lost the sun in their lives. Grant them the comfort of Your Holy Spirit and the assurance that one day their sun will shine again.

*Sun of my soul, Thou Saviour dear;*
*It is not night if Thou be near:*
*O may no earth-born cloud arise*
*To hide Thee from Thy servant's eyes.*

*John Keble*

* * *

# 18th May

Therefore do not be foolish, but understand what the Lord's will is.

Ephesians 5:17

*To know Thy will, Lord of the seeking mind,*
*To learn Thy way for me, Thy purpose kind,*
*Thy path to follow and Thy guide find –*
*For this I pray.*

*To do Thy will, Lord of the eager soul,*
*To bring my restlessness 'neath Thy control,*
*To give Thee, not a part, but all – the whole –*
*For this I pray.*

*To love Thy will, Lord of the ardent heart,*
*To bid all selfishness, all sloth depart,*
*To share with gladness all Thou dost and art –*
*For this I pray.*

*Alice M. Kyle*

Show me Your ways O Lord, teach me Your paths,
Guide me in Your truth and teach me for You are
God my Saviour,
And my hope is in You all day long.

Psalm 25:4–5

* * *

# 19th May

The next day we set sail from Mitylene and arrived off Chios. The day after that we crossed over to Samos and on the following day arrived in Miletus.

Acts 20:15

Luke jotted down his travelogue in just the way you or I might send our postcards home – though we have the advantage of more reliable boats! Nevertheless, there is no guarantee what the sea will be like and, more than we realise, some owe their lives to the rescue services. A week-end sailor set sail, but with lack of experience and concentration didn't realise that his boat was drifting. Only when he looked back to a point on the coast did he recognise the danger of his position. And we, too, caught up in new excitements can all too soon drift helplessly away from our Lighthouse, our Captain, our God.

*Eternal Father, strong to save,*
*Whose arm doth bind the restless wave. . . .*
*O hear us when we cry to Thee*
*For those in peril on the sea.*

*William Whiting*

* * *

# 20th May

So Ruth went out and began to glean in the fields behind the harvesters. As it turned out she found herself working in a field belonging to Boaz. Just then Boaz arrived from Bethlehem and greeted the harvesters: 'The Lord be with you.'

'The Lord bless you!' they called back.

Boaz asked the foreman of his harvesters, 'Whose young woman is that?'

The foreman replied, 'She is the Moabitess who came back from Moab with Naomi. She said, "Please let me glean and gather among the sheaves behind the harvesters". She went into the field and has worked steadily from morning till now, except for a short rest in the shelter.'

So Boaz said to Ruth, 'My daughter, listen to me. Don't go and glean in another field and don't go away from here. Stay here with my servant girls. Watch the field where the men are harvesting, and follow along after the girls. I have told the men not to touch you. And whenever you are thirsty go and get a drink from the water jars the men have filled.'. . . . 'I have been told all about what you have done for your mother-in-law since your husband died. . . . May the Lord repay you for what you have done.'

Ruth 2:4–12

* * *

# 21st May

Jesus said: 'Go home to your family and tell them how much the Lord has done for you.'

Mark 5:19

Most people have forgotten nowadays what a home can mean, though some of us have come to realise it as never before. It is a kingdom of its own in the midst of the world, a haven or refuge amid the turmoil of our age. It is not founded on the shifting sands of private and public life, but has its peace in God. For it is God who gave it its special meaning and dignity, its nature and privilege, its destiny and worth. It is an ordinance God has established in the world, the place where peace, quietness, joy, love, purity, continence, respect, obedience, tradition and, to crown them all, happiness may dwell, whatever else may pass away in the world. It is the woman's calling and her joy to build up this world within the world for her husband. . . .

Dietrich Bonhoeffer

*Happy the home where man and wife together*
*Are of one mind believing in your love:*
*Through love and pain, prosperity and hardship*
*Through good and evil days your care they prove.*

*Karl Spitta*

* * *

# 22nd May

. . . when he rules in the fear of God, he is like the light of morning at sunrise on a cloudless morning. . . .

2 Samuel 23:7

There is nothing quite so crisp, pure and envigorating as the sight of the sun rising on a cloudless morning. King David, in his last words, recognised that justice has this same quality – this bright spearhead illuminating the darkness of human sin. Lord, I pray for all those who suffer today the twilight of injustice, the night of fear . . . those who are burdened and see no dawn in view. . . . I pray for myself, for justice in my dealings with others, for openness and a bright attitude which reflects the Sun of Righteousness.

*The star of morn has risen:*
*O Lord, to Thee we pray,*
*O uncreated Light of Light,*
*Guide Thou our way.*

*Anon. c. 8th century.*

* * *

# 23rd May

Joy and gladness will be found (in Zion), thanksgiving and the sound of singing.

Isaiah 51:3

*Thank God for life, for living*
*Thank God for love, for giving*
*Thank God for death – an ending a beginning . . .*

*Thank God for lips, for speaking*
*Thank God for hearts, for seeking*
*Thank God for weakness – a stumbling an upsurging.*

*Thank God for eyes, for seeing*
*Thank God for soul, for being*
*Thank God for absence – a longing an unfolding . . .*

*Thank God for life, for loving,*
*Thank God for death, for longing*
*Thank Him with singing.*

*Mary E. Morgan, Jamaica*

Some people are never satisfied with what they have. But what a difference it makes when we realise that everything we have has been given to us by God.

Billy Graham

* * *

# 24th May

Therefore, since we have been justified through faith, we have peace with God through our Lord Jesus Christ.

Romans 5:1

The last sentence spoken by John Wesley was 'the best is God is with us!' John Wesley whose heart was strangely warmed on 24 May 1738 was totally convinced that God was always with him and in that peace he was content to die. When I say, 'God is with us', who do I mean by 'us'? My circle of friends? Those of the same background? Those who share my beliefs? Lord, widen my horizons – like John Wesley, let me feel the whole world is part of my experience and prayer concern, and not only the whole world but the great company of saints on earth and in heaven. God is with us all!

*God be in my head and in my understanding*
*God be at my end and at my departing.*

*From Sarum Primer*

* * *

# 25th May

As the deer pants for streams of water, so my soul pants for You, O God.

Psalm 42:1

*As the deer pants for the water*
*So my soul longs after You.*
*You alone are my heart's desire*
*And I long to worship You.*

*I want You more than gold or silver*
*Only You can satisfy*
*You alone are the real joy-giver*
*And the apple of my eye.*

*You are my Friend and You are my Brother*
*Even though You are a King.*
*I love You more than any other*
*So much more than anything.*

*Martin Nystrom*

By day the Lord directs His love, at night His song is with me – a prayer to the God of my life.

Psalm 42:8

* * *

# 26th May

Bring an offering and come before Him; worship the Lord in the beauty of His holiness.

1 Chronicles 16:29

You've made the world so beautiful, Lord, let me take time to see it. Even as I'm rushing to the market or driving the children to their destinations, let me be aware of it; the glory of hills and woods and shining water. The colours of traffic lights and buses, of fruit stands and lumberyards . . . let me lift my eyes from the dishes to rejoice in the sunshine spilling through the trees. . . . In the raindrops strung out on the clothes line like a string of crystal beads. Let me take time for beauty, Lord.

Marjorie Holmes

*O worship the Lord in the beauty of holiness!*
*Truth in its beauty and love in its tenderness,*
*These are the offerings to lay on His shrine.*

*J. S. B. Monsell*

* * *

# 27th May

In my former book, I wrote about all that Jesus began to do and teach until He was taken up to heaven, after giving instructions through the Holy Spirit to the apostles He had chosen. After His suffering He showed Himself to these men and gave many convincing proofs that He was alive. He appeared to them over a period of forty days and spoke about the Kingdom of God. On one occasion, while He was eating with them, he gave them this command: 'Do not leave Jerusalem but wait for the gift my Father promised, which you have heard me speak about. For John baptised with water, but in a few days you will be baptised with the Holy Spirit.'

So when they met together, they asked Him,

'Lord, are you at this time going to restore the kingdom to Israel?'

He said to them: 'It is not for you to know the times or dates the Father has set by his own authority. But you will receive power when the Holy Spirit comes on you; and you will be my witness in Jerusalem, and in all Judea and Samaria, and to the ends of the earth.'

After He said this, He was taken up before their very eyes, and a cloud hid Him from their sight.

Acts 1:1–9

* * *

# 28th May

In Him was life, and that life was the light of men.

John 1:4

The other day I saw the sea, calm and serene. The waves came from afar . . . quietly holding hands, they slipped noiselessly and stretched at full length on the sand, to touch the shore with the tips of their beautiful fingers. The sun gently caressed them and they generously returned streams of light. . . .

Give my face the light of clear waters.

Give my soul the whiteness of foam.

Illumine my life that it may sing like sunbeams on the surface of the sea. But above all, Lord, may I not keep this light for myself, and may all those who come near me return home eager to bathe in Your eternal grace.

Michel Quoist

*O Light that followest all my way . . .*
*My heart restores its borrowed ray*
*That in Thy sunshine's blaze its day*
*May brighter, fairer be.*

*George Matheson*

* * *

# 29th May

The apostles gathered round Jesus and reported to Him all they had done and taught.

Mark 6:30

I believe in God, the Father Almighty, creator of heaven and earth. I believe in Jesus Christ, His only Son our Lord. He was conceived by the power of the Holy Spirit and born of the Virgin Mary. He suffered under Pontius Pilate was crucified, died, and was buried. He descended to the dead. On the third day He rose again. He ascended into heaven, and is seated at the right hand of the Father. He will come again to judge the living and the dead.

I believe in the Holy Spirit, the holy catholic Church, the communion of saints, the forgiveness of sins, the resurrection of the body and the life everlasting. Amen.

The Apostles' Creed

* * *

# 30th May

Continue to work out your salvation with fear and trembling, for it is God who works in you.

Philippians 2:12

For so much of my life, I really wanted to be pleasing God, and I tried to 'work out my own salvation', and I'm afraid there was a lot of fear and trembling, and finally a sense of hopelessness and failure about it. I was trying to be 'good' with my own resources and good intentions – and it just didn't work. I finally read the next verse in Philippians and began to understand it, and it has changed my life and given me hope and confidence for eternity. I see now that God is willing to do it all, if I'll just allow Him to! I finally invited Him to dwell in me by His Holy Spirit, and cause me to want to do the right things . . . what a sadness that only those who have experienced it can really understand it.

Pat Boone

*Therefore my dear friends, as you have always obeyed, continue to work out your salvation with fear and trembling for it is God who works in you to will and to act according to His good purpose.*

*Philippians 2:12–13*

* * *

# 31st May

Jesus said: 'Whoever wants to be great among you must be your servant, and whosoever wants to be first must be a slave to all.'

Mark 10:43–44

*Lord of all pots and pans and things*
*Since I've no time to be*
*A saint by doing lovely things*
*Or watching late with thee:*
*Or dreaming in the dawn light;*
*Or storming heaven's gates –*
*Make me a saint by getting meals*
*And washing up the plates.*

*Fay Inchfawn*

Jesus said: 'For even the Son of Man did not come to be served but to serve, and to give His life as a ransom for many.'

Mark 10:46

* * *

# 1st June

Let us not become weary of doing good . . .

Galatians 6:9

The Indians have an interesting thought that it is always a privilege to help a Brahman, even a Brahman beggar, because you are helping a man in whom God dwells more fully than in any other caste. Jesus, it seems to me, would teach, a similar thought, that it is always a privilege to help anybody, because all men are of the same caste, the very highest caste. They are all sons of God. They are men in whom God dwells. And, indeed, I think it is not poetic fancy merely, but the naked truth.

Dr Leslie Weatherhead

*We have no mission but to serve*
*In full obedience to our Lord;*
*To care for all, without reserve*
*And spread His liberating word.*

*F. Pratt-Green*

* * *

# 2nd June

God has raised this Jesus to life, and we are all witnesses to the fact.

Acts 2:32

God alive! He could miraculously heal today, speak through men today. This was not a story about people who lived in a different and remote period of history. It was about today. It was about people who lived in semi-detached houses, and went to the office, and had mortgages to pay, and liked pop music, and wore denims, played squash at the local leisure centre, and found the boss a pain in the neck.

If this was for real – it was for me.

Gerald Williams
after hearing a sermon by Colin Urquhart

*Christ is alive! No longer bound*
*To distant years in Palestine,*
*He comes to claim the here and now*
*And conquer every place and time.*

*Brian A. Wren*

* * *

# 3rd June

When the day of Pentecost came, they were all together in one place. Suddenly a sound like the blowing of a violent wind came from heaven and filled the whole house where they were sitting. They saw what seemed to be tongues of fire that separated and came to rest on each of them. All of them were filled with the Holy Spirit and began to speak in other tongues as the Spirit enabled them.

Now there were staying in Jerusalem, God-fearing Jews from every nation under heaven. When they heard this sound, a crowd came together in bewilderment, because each one heard them speaking in his own language. Utterly amazed, they asked: 'Are not all these men who are speaking Galileans? Then how is it each of us hears them in his own native language? Parthians, Medes and Elamites; residents of Mesopotamia, Judea and Cappadocia, Pontus and Asia, Phrygia and Pamphylia, Egypt and the parts of Libya near Cyrene; visitors from Rome, Cretans and Arabs – we hear them declaring the wonders of God in our own tongues!'

Amazed and perplexed, they asked one another, 'What does this mean?'

Acts 2:1–12

* * *

# 4th June

At that time Mary got ready and hurried to a town in the hill country of Judah, where she entered Zechariah's home and greeted Elizabeth.

Luke 1:39

It must have been a pretty special friendship between Mary and Elizabeth – and, indeed, there is an automatic bond between two women as they share the joys, uncertainties and excitement of a first pregnancy. Suddenly we find ourselves in situations where there is so much to learn and not nearly enough time to do so. It's then that we need the love and encouragement of someone who has either been through our experience or is actually sharing it along with us. Lord, help me to see that I am not the first person to feel as I do . . . and I shall not be the last! And if I can help someone else by my own experience, give me courage to grasp the opportunity.

*Like Mary, let us ponder in our mind*
*God's wondrous love . . .*

* * *

# 5th June

If God is for us – who can be against us?

Romans 8:31

You know and I know the gospel message is as great today as it has ever been. This is God's work and I believe that Jesus is His Son. I believe that Jesus lives and is among us and that nothing happens to us but that His healing touch can give us the strength we need for every experience in life. It's good to know that God Almighty is along with us because His Holy Spirit is our strength.

George Thomas: Lord Tonypandy

*Speed the cross through all the nations*
*Speed the victories of love,*
*Preach the gospel of redemption*
*Wheresoever men may move:*
*God is with us; God is with us*
*Christ our Lord shall reign as King.*

*W. J. Mathams*

* * *

# 6th June

. . . the people that know their God shall be strong.

Daniel 11:32

This verse tells us not what a great man can do for God, but what our great God can do through any man or woman who is available to Him. May God give us the dauntless spirit of Luther, the iron courage of John Knox, the holy indignation of Savonarola, and the spiritual power of Elijah, all of whom protested loudly by lip and by life when they saw the corruption of their day. May we have grace to serve God all our days.

Francis W. Dixon

*Stand up, stand up for Jesus*
*Stand in His strength alone:*
*The arm of flesh will fail you*
*Ye dare not trust your own.*

*George Duffield*

* * *

# 7th June

Jesus said: 'If anyone would come after me, he must deny himself and take up his cross and follow me.'

Matthew 16:24

Merrell Vories had ambitions to be an architect. But the hand of God guided him from his native America to Japan in the early days of this century where he determined to prove that Christianity makes a far bigger impact where it is talked the least – lived the most. His life was indeed one of the most remarkable missionary adventures of the past hundred years and well worth reading. The Brotherhood he founded, after taking Japanese nationality, was a miracle of intercultural co-operation and Merrell emphasised the importance of how and why the Brotherhood lived and worked as they did. He said the Brotherhood was not an argument for Christianity – it was a demonstration!

*Democracy is co-operation. Is it not significant that even our Japanese character for the word 'co-operation' has a Christian cross at its centre.*

*Merrell Vories explaining Christian Democracy to the Emperor of Japan.*

* * *

# 8th June

Jesus said: 'And why do you worry about clothes? See how the lilies of the field grow . . . I tell you that not even Solomon in all his splendour was dressed like one of these.'

Matthew 6:28–29

The skill of drying flowers is becoming a popular craft – a spring and summer occupation of collecting specimens ensures busy winter evenings creating pictures, birthday cards and bookmarks for friends and family. Yet however well the petals dry, they are but a shadow of their living glory. We pretend they are everlasting but they are not: we cannot prolong their beauty nor capture their perfume. Flowers are transient as we are – I am not able to prolong a perfect hour or hasten a painful minute. Lord, give me the ability to enjoy the moments I have to the full – memories can be locked away and treasured but it is the 'now' that is truly precious.

*Dear Mother Earth, who day by day*
*Unfoldest blessings on our way,*
*O praise Him, Alleluia!*
*The flowers and fruits that in thee grow*
*Let them His glory also show*
*O praise Him, Alleluia, Alleluia.*

*St Francis of Assissi*

* * *

# 9th June

Remember how the Lord your God led you all the way . . .

Deuteronomy 8:2

I believe that God does guide us, without a doubt. The way I see it, the basic Christian commitment is to tell God you want to do things His way, not your own in future. You believe He has heard and answered that prayer, and so you accept whatever comes as being His will for you. If God has promised to guide His people (and He has) then if you sincerely want to do His will He does guide you even when it doesn't seem like it.

Cliff Richard

*Lead us, Heavenly Father, lead us*
*O'er the world's tempestuous sea;*
*Guard us, guide us, keep us, feed us,*
*For we have no help but Thee.*

*James Edmeston*

* * *

# 10th June

When they saw the courage of Peter and John and realised that they were unschooled, ordinary men, they were astonished and took note that these men had been with Jesus. But since they could see the man who had been healed standing there with them, there was nothing they could say. So they ordered them to withdraw from the Sanhedrin and then conferred together.

'What are we going to do with these men?' they asked.

'Everybody living in Jerusalem knows they have done an outstanding miracle, and we cannot deny it. But to stop this thing from spreading any further among the people, we must warn these men to speak no longer to anyone in this name.'

Then they called them in again and commanded them not to speak or teach at all in the name of Jesus. But Peter and John replied: 'We cannot help speaking about what we have seen and heard.'

Acts 4:13–18 & 20

* * *

# 11th June

'What are those feeble Jews doing? Will they restore their wall?'. . . . So we rebuilt the wall . . . for the people worked with all their heart.

Nehemiah 4:2 & 6

It's a strange reality that people give of their best when the chips are down – or in the case of the Jews, the walls! In the face of opposition and derision, the Jews all pulled together, got stuck in with heart and soul and rebuilt the wall around Jerusalem. Today there are other kinds of walls that need rebuilding . . . lives have been broken and it might seem that they can never be restored. But take heart, it can be done! Come to Jesus, the cornerstone, trust in Him, and allow His followers to pick up the pieces, rebuild the broken-hearted, restore the bruised and shattered. Lord the tools are there help me to put my heart into the task.

*Son of the carpenter, enable all young people with vision, courage, confidence and skills; may they live productive lives with their self-worth and dignity enhanced; may they become living stones in the house of God; unite us all in You, the chief cornerstone.*

*Bill Watty*

* * *

# 12th June

Great is the Lord and most worthy of praise.

Psalm 48:1

I once read a book containing a practical plan for personalised prayer which divided up an hour into prayer segments.

The advice was that the hour of prayer should begin and end on the level of praise. For most of us, our immediate prayers are all wrapped up in five or ten minutes so that a whole hour seems somewhat daunting at first. But let me pass on the menu of this hour and you may like to give it a try: praise; silent waiting; confession; Scripture praying; develop holy alertness; remember needs of the world; share personal needs; thanksgiving; worship with song; meditate; listen; and praise. Each ingredient takes five minutes . . . suddenly an hour seems hardly long enough!

*When morning guilds the skies*
*My heart awaking cries*
*May Jesus Christ be praised!*
*Alike at work and prayer*
*To Jesus I repair*
*May Jesus Christ be praised!*

*Anon*

* * *

# 13th June

The city streets will be filled with boys and girls playing there . . .

Zechariah 8:5

The Lord spoke through the prophet Zechariah of the eventual return of the Jews to Jerusalem – a wonderful dream for the exiles to cling to as they yearned to hear the streets of their Holy City ringing with the laughter and play of their children in peace and security. A dream that has never been truly fulfilled either in Jerusalem or in any other city. Danger lurks to dampen the laughter. Violence, fear of abduction, traffic or disease goes hand-in-hand with their games. Lord, Loving Father of all your children, I pray for true peace, for the joy of innocent children at play.

*In the streets of every city*
*Where the bruised and lonely dwell*
*Let us show the Saviour's pity,*
*Let us of His mercy tell.*

*Light for darkness, joy for sorrow –*
*Love for hatred – peace for strife.*

*Hugh Sherlock*

* * *

# 14th June

One of those days Jesus went out into the hills to pray, and spent the night praying to God.

Luke 6:12

Prayer is one of the most under-rated activities and therefore a discipline that has been neglected by too many followers of Jesus. Even His own disciples fell asleep over their prayers! Thank You, Lord, that there are people who are still prepared to have all-night prayer sessions for needy areas in life. Give them strength, give me the desire if not to join them all night, at least to up-grade my praying. Help me to realise that people are actually helped when they know they are being lifted up in prayer. Prayer is indeed the way of reaching out to my Lord when I can't do anything else physically or practically.

*For me, the life of prayer is very important. A way of experiencing God's power. I would like to thank God for all who follow Christ and spread His message through all the world.*

*Bishop Armando Rodrigues of Cuba*

* * *

# 15th June

Christ is the image of the invisible God . . .

Colossians 1:15

*World Children's Day*: Mother Frances Dominica, the founder of the first-ever hospice for children, spoke on television about one little boy's attitude to his own death. He called his body his reflection, something he would leave behind when he died because he wouldn't need it any more.

'But,' the lad added with the clarity and trust given only to children, 'the real me won't die!' Surely, out of the mouth of that young boy came the Gospel of truth and hope for young and old. Lord, today my prayers are for children everywhere – the sick and the strong, the black and the white – Your children, Lord . . . our hope.

*Immortal, invisible God only wise.*

* * *

# 16th June

> Water will gush forth in the wilderness and streams in the desert.
>
> Isaiah 35:6

*The mind rests on the edge of a gliding stream –*
*waiting for the impetus that carries through into midstream –*
*Like a boat following the 'pull' of the current*
*Music and pictures are in themselves relaxing –*
*And carry the mind away from the centre of self,*
*Enjoying afresh a sense of wonder in God's creation –*
*Steeping the worshipper in praise and adoration –*
*Leading us to our need for forgiveness –*
*Calling us to a sense of responsibility – and to service for God.*

*June Lunn*

God calls us in so many ways . . . every day we receive visual images of sunrises, streams, trees, creatures, children. . . . How can we use them as springboards for prayer? Today, Lord, please accept the stream of all my thoughts and hopes as my prayer, and may they merge in Your streams of Living Water.

* * *

# 17th June

Stephen accused: 'You stiff-necked people! . . . You are just like your fathers: you always resist the Holy Spirit! Was there ever a prophet your fathers did not persecute? They even killed those who predicted the coming of the Righteous One. And now you have betrayed and murdered Him.'

When they heard this they were furious and gnashed their teeth at him. But Stephen, full of the Holy Spirit, looked up to heaven and saw the glory of God and Jesus standing at the right hand of God.

'Look,' he said, 'I see heaven open and the Son of Man standing at the right hand of God.'

At this, they covered their ears and, yelling at the top of their voices, they all rushed at him, dragged him out of the city and began to stone him.

Meanwhile, the witnesses laid their clothes at the feet of a young man named Saul.

Acts 7:51–58

* * *

# 18th June

You are no longer foreigners and aliens, but fellow-citizens with God's people and members of God's household.

Recently, a delegation from churches in Thailand visited the churches in Burma, our next-door neighbour. A Burmese woman in the audience sang for us a song about December and January. These two months stand next to each other, but on the calendar they are also far from each other. We all realized the point: though we are Christians living in countries which are next-door neighbours, we are far apart. Very often Christians do not realise that through Christ we are one. Even if we live far apart, we are fellow-citizens of the household of God. When we allow divisions such as race and denomination to exist, we stay far from each other when we could be near.

Pornwadee Arkkapin (Bangkok, Thailand)

*Still we are centred all in Thee*
*Members, though distant, of one Head:*
*In the same family we be,*
*By the same faith and spirit led.*

*Richard Baxter (1615–1691)*

* * *

# 19th June

Festus interrupted Paul's defence. 'You are out of your mind, Paul,' he shouted. 'Your great learning is driving you insane!'

Act 26:24

For me, the word that gives this scene its ring of utter authenticity is the word 'shouted'. Festus was wound up! He couldn't bear the arguments and witness that Paul was giving so he resorted to a fairly common accusation: 'You're mad!'

However, praise God that for so many it is these same arguments and personal witness that keep people sane! Roger Augue, a Frenchman, was held hostage in the Lebanon for nearly a year. He records, 'The one who gave me a Bible did me a blessed service; being able to read the Bible kept me sane.'

*Lord, strengthen the will and faith of all those who are imprisoned for their belief, or their conscience or held hostage. I pray for them in their isolation and for their loved ones in heart-breaking separation and helplessness . . . may Your justice rule the earth.*

* * *

# 20th June

When Priscilla and Aquila heard him (Apollos) they invited him to their home and explained to him the way of God more adequately.

Acts 18:26

Earlier in the eighteenth chapter of Acts we read that this Jewish couple, Aquila and Priscilla, were Italians from Rome, and had fled to the cosmopolitan city of Corinth when the Roman Emperor had ordered all the Jews to leave Rome. They were a good, solid team. They worked together as tent-makers, they worshipped together in the synagogue and they entertained and discussed together their new-found faith in Jesus Christ. Oh, that there were more husbands and wives so closely bound together in every aspect of living! Lord, give me courage to witness for Jesus, deepen my faith that I can explain Him to others in my home or anywhere, and may the bonds of love and partnership in marriage be a right reflection of the bonds between Christ and His church.

*Lord of love and life,*
*Blessing man and wife,*
*As they stand, their need confessing*
*May your hand take theirs in blessing*
*You will share their life;*
*Bless this man and wife.*

*Basil E. Bridge*

* * *

# 21st June

As Jesus walked beside the Sea of Galilee, he saw Simon and his brother Andrew casting a net into the lake, for they were fishermen. 'Come, follow me!' Jesus said.

Mark 1:16

*Heavenly Father lead our church,*
*Self-governing, self-supporting, self-propagating,*
*Magnifying the Lord's light.*
*Standing steadfast in the East,*
*Jesus our leader, we will always follow.*

*Heavenly Father lead our church,*
*One Lord, one faith, one baptism,*
*Spreading Christ, lifting high the cross,*
*The Holy Spirit in work, we will always follows.*

*We love Christ's church in China*
*The church is a golden lantern,*
*Uniting into one, loving one another;*
*The Lord is always with us.*
*Translation of a hymn by Shi Qi-gui and Sun Ding-wu*

Lord, help me never to forget the millions of believers of different cultures and colours and languages – the miracle of Your uniting spirit to make us one in Jesus, our corporate aim to follow Him.

* * *

# 22nd June

> 'I'm going out to fish,' Simon Peter told them, and they said, 'We'll go with you.' So they went out and got into the boat, but that night they caught nothing.
>
> John 21:3

It's not hard to imagine the group of men whom Jesus had called from fishing to become His disciples, huddled together not quite knowing what to do next – they don't know whether they are on their heads or heels – the sight of the risen Master had thrilled them beyond belief, but He was not with them all the time, they just did not understand. Into this unreal atmosphere comes Peter's voice: 'I'm going out to fish!' We all get to a point where we don't know what to do but we can't sit around moping or staring at each other . . . what a good idea to go and busy themselves at what they knew best. Lord, there is always something for me to do . . . guide me.

*Loving heavenly Father, creator and provider of all fish in rivers, lakes, seas and oceans, I pray for those who fish to eat, who fish to earn a living, who fish to find peace of mind. My prayer is also for the fishers of men and women, boys and girls in so many areas of need. Lord, bless us all.*

* * *

# 23rd June

> Jesus called out to them: 'Friends, have you any fish?' 'No,' they answered.
>
> John 21:5

Yesterday we thought about the disconsolate fishermen; today we can read that instead of having a good night's fishing and activity, they saw the dawn rise on empty nets – it seemed they had wasted their time! Yes, indeed, we do waste our time if we stamp off to undertake things in our own strength, but to listen and obey the voice of Jesus on our lives is to transform our situation. No experience is ever a waste of time if we give it to the Lord of Life.

> *The Galilean fishers toil all night and nothing take:*
> *But Jesus comes – a wondrous spoil is lifted from the lake!*
> *Lord, when our labours are in vain and vain the help of men,*
> *When fruitless is our care and pain . . .*
> *Come, blessed Jesus then.*
>
> *Christopher Wordsworth*

* * *

# 24th June

> Then I saw a new heaven and a new earth, for the first heaven and the first earth had passed away, and there was no longer any sea. I saw the Holy City, the new Jerusalem, coming down out of

heaven from God, prepared as a bride beautifully dressed for her husband. And I heard a loud voice from the throne saying, 'Now the dwelling of God is with men, and He will live with them. They will be His people and God Himself will be with them and be their God. He will wipe every tear from their eyes. There will be no more death or mourning or crying or pain, for the old order of things has passed away.' He who was seated on the throne said, 'I am making everything new!' . . . 'I am the Alpha and the Omega, the beginning and the end.'

Revelation 21:1–6

* * *

# 25th June

And by Him we cry 'Abba, Father'. The Spirit himself testifies with our spirit that we are God's children.

Romans 8:15

*His Spirit answers to the blood*
*And tells me I am born of God.*

*He owns me for His child –*
*His pardoning voice I hear;*
*In Jesus reconciled*
*I can no longer fear.*
*With confidence I now draw nigh*
*And, 'Father, Abba, Father' cry.*

*Charles Wesley*

It's a long time, Lord, since I was a child – a long time since I gave way to trembling fear and uncertainty, to weakness and lack of knowledge. But as I sink in prayer now, all those feelings flood into my heart and mind . . . I am vulnerable, I need love and guidance. I need to feel my Father's arms bearing me into a new day.

* * *

# 26th June

> On Herod's birthday the daughter of Herodias danced for them and pleased Herod so much that he promised with an oath to give her whatever she asked.
>
> Matthew 14:6

Herod's birthday party ended up with the murder of John the Baptist. We can imagine the sleazy scene painted so vividly in so few sentences – the drinking and the dancing, the boasting and the swearing and the lechery, the every day story of people then and now! The object lesson here is how dangerous is the tongue when fuelled with alcohol and lust – when people let power carry them away and pride prevents a climbdown. Herod had no intention of beheading John at the beginning of the evening – he was afraid of the public reaction: but with drink inside him his common sense and decency deserted him.

*Lord I pray for those who are ruled by alcohol – who turn from being kind, thoughtful husbands and wives into violent, deceitful strangers. I pray for the families that have been ruined by drink – lives lost through accidents or vicious attacks, for all those in fear. Lord, may they find comfort from those who love You.*

* * *

# 27th June

> God said to Moses: 'I am the God of your father, the God of Abraham, the God of Isaac and the God of Jacob.'
>
> Exodus 3:6

Little Tommy was orphaned at the age of four. As he grew, he became an unruly, rebellious youth and got himself into debt and bad company. However, quite unexpectedly, during his apprenticeship to a shoemaker, Tommy heard the great preacher George Whitefield and experienced a dramatic conversion. He joined the Methodists and became a sub-editor of one of their magazines. John Wesley was much taken with Thomas Olivers, the volatile little Welshman whose life had been transformed by the gospel of love, and one of Thomas' poems became a stirring hymn of praise.

*The God of Abraham praise,*
*Who reigns enthroned above,*
*Ancient of everlasting days,*
*And God of love.*
*Jehovah! Great I am!*
*By earth and heaven confessed.*
*I bow and bless the sacred name*
*For ever blessed.*

*Thomas Olivers*

* * *

# 28th June

And I pray that you may grasp how wide and long and high and deep is the love of Christ, and to know this love that surpasses knowledge . . .

Ephesians 3:19

For most of her 56 years, Ireland's Mary Shekleton was a chronic invalid. But not for her the attitude of 'there's nothing I can do'. Mary devoted her life to working for many charities and she founded the Invalids' Prayer Union, thus proving how vital prayer can be in uniting Christians who are able-bodied or physically weak and handicapped. The love of Christ is so high and deep that it encompasses everybody, young and old, the fit and the sick. Lord, if I need inspiration today, I only have to look at the achievements of those who suffer from illness and handicap . . . their faith, perseverance and enthusiasm makes me ashamed.

*It passeth knowledge that dear love of Thine*
*My Saviour Jesus, yet this soul of mine*
*Would of Thy love in all its breadth and length*
*Its height and depth and everlasting strength*
*Know more and more.*

*Mary Shekleton*

* * *

# 29th June

As they talked and discussed these things with each other, Jesus himself came up and walked along with them.

Luke 24:15

I am persuaded that God is greater than logic, though not contrary to logic, and our mere inability to catch Him in the little net of our human reason is no proof of His non-existence, but only of our need that our little reason shall be supplemented by His tender visitations, and that He may lead and guide us to the end of the road in ways superior to any that our intellects can plan. This is the blindness of trust, which walks with Him, unafraid, into the dark.

Thomas R. Kelly

*So shall my walk be close with God*
*Calm and serene my frame;*
*So purer light shall mark the road*
*That leads me to the Lamb.*

*William Cowper*

* * *

# 30th June

Jesus said: 'Are not two sparrows sold for a penny? . . .'

Matthew 10:29

It's amusing to notice the commercial aspect which Jesus brought in to his conversations . . . in Matthew's gospel we read of two sparrows sold for a farthing whilst in Luke we read of the better bargain of five sparrows for two farthings! So Jesus comes right into our High Street mentality, offering us the eternal truth that in any throw-away, consumer society individuals can feel lost and rejected, but God the loving Father knows and cares for the least of us. And so, if God cares, I must care, for I am part of the society which sets such faith in possessions. Help me Lord to witness to my greatest possession – my unshakeable faith in the risen Christ.

*He sees the meanest sparrow fall unnoticed . . .*
*Almighty Father, Lover of the meek,*
*Make me a friend of the helpless and the weak.*

* * *

# 1st July

But where can wisdom be found? Where does understanding dwell? Man does not comprehend its worth; it cannot be found in the land of the living. The deep says 'It's not in me' the sea says 'It is not with me'. It cannot be bought with the finest gold, nor can its price be weighed in silver . . . Coral and jasper are not worthy of mention; the price of wisdom is beyond rubies. Where then does wisdom come from? Where does understanding dwell? God understands the way to it and He alone knows where it dwells, for He views the ends of the earth and sees everything under the heavens. And He said: 'The fear of the Lord – that is wisdom: and to shun evil is understanding.'

Job 28:12–15, 18, 23, 28.

* * *

# 2nd July

Go out to the roads and the country lanes . . .

Luke 14:23

There is a heady scent in a sheltered country lane. Like some gigantic fabric print, hedges are dotted with multicoloured flowers in amongst the nettles, ferns and grasses. Yellow, pink, purple, white, honeysuckle and roses tumbling in a summer tangle along the road. No one has busied themselves in pruning, organic feeding, protecting against frost and pest – I see in front of me the richness of free nature. Lord, I love to go into the country lanes, to walk, to linger, to quietly acknowledge Your creation . . . the shades and scents which only walking can realise. Thank You, Lord.

*Those little lanes they have not changed,*
*A sweet peace fills the air:*
*I walked today where Jesus walked*
*And felt His presence there.*

*Daniel S. Twohig*

* * *

# 3rd July

Then God said: 'Let us make man in our image . . . and let them rule over the fish of the sea and the birds of the air, over the livestock, over all the earth. . . .'

Genesis 1:26

My whole life is filled with the glory of creative evolution for I have been given the opportunity to use the one 'talent' (the power of conscious thought) which sets man apart from all the products of creative evolution, to try to understand the meaning of that dominion. To fail to understand is of little consequence, but to fail to use that one talent and strive to understand is failure indeed. . . . The world is a marvellous place, thank God; He set the process of creative evolution in motion and placed the power of creation within the dominion of our thinking minds and dextrous hands.

David Bellamy

*Jesus is Lord, creation's voice proclaims it,*
*For, by His power, each tree and flower*
*Was planned and made.*

*David J. Mansell*

* * *

# 4th July

The same Lord is Lord of all . . . for everyone who calls on the name of the Lord will be saved.

Romans 10:12–13

It is one of the great tragedies of the Christian life that very often those whose faith is strongest and most 'evangelical' are quickest to accuse others of heresy, of modernism, of liberalism, and to insist that anyone who has not had the same experience as they have had has had no Christian experience at all. There are – blessed be God! – many ways to God. No man has any monopoly of belief or of experience.

William Barclay

*He is Lord! He is Lord!*
*He is risen from the dead and He is Lord!*
*Every knee shall bow, every tongue confess*
*That Jesus Christ is Lord!*

*Anon*

* * *

# 5th July

But if you harbour bitter envy and selfish ambition in your hearts, do not boast about it or deny the truth.

James 3:14

The cottages in the village street were picture-postcard whitewash and thatch. A stranger knocked at the door of one to ask the way to the Chapel. The woman stood in the doorway and instead of giving directions, lambasted the Chapelgoers for not visiting her when her husband had died: no one had bothered with her, and she certainly wasn't going to bother with them! When the widow had finally run out of bitter steam, the stranger softly asked if she had ever visited anyone in the village when they had suffered bereavement. . . . It had never occurred to the woman to treat others in the way she craved to be treated. She was living without Love.

*Come to my heart O thou wonderful love*
*Come and abide:*
*Lifting my life till it rises above*
*Envy, and falsehood and pride!*

*Robert Walmsley*

* * *

# 6th July

God has said: Never will I leave you: never will I forsake you.

Hebrews 13:5

I was once stuck in a lift. My companion, terrified, turned pale and looked desperate. I don't much like being stuck in lifts either, but my overwhelming desire at that moment was to relieve her great fear, and, as you may have noticed, when someone else is afraid it can make one braver. I said: 'Wherever we are, we are always in the same place – whether we are in a lift, on or under ground, in the air, on or in the sea, in or out of buildings.' By which I meant that as the spiritual child of God one can never, for a fraction of a second, be outside His encompassing Love. I knew God had not singled me out to receive a good idea when it was needed, for His supply of good ideas is infinite and always available to everyone.

Joyce Grenfell

*I know not where His islands lift*
*Their fronded palms in air:*
*I only know I cannot drift*
*Beyond His love and care.*

*J. G. Whittier*

* * *

# 7th July

Then, because so many people were coming and going that they did not even have a chance to eat, Jesus said to them, 'Come with me by yourselves to a quiet place and get some rest'.

Mark 6:31

I suppose every public figure would agree that the mass of people are totally inconsiderate. The public figure is expected to 'perform' non-stop, and it seems the same was true of the public expectations of Jesus. They crowded to where He was, clammering for attention, healing, teaching. . . . Jesus made it plain – time off is essential. Lack of time off leads to inefficiency, anxiety and exhaustion, but so often we tell ourselves that we are indispensable. It is a hard truth to swallow that the world will not crumble if we take a rest. . . . Lord, help me to organise my time to make the best of time for work and for leisure . . . give me time for people and time for You.

*There is a place of quiet rest*
*Near to the heart of God –*
*O Jesus, blest Redeemer, sent from the heart of God*
*Hold us who wait before You, near to the heart of God.*

*C. B. MacAfee*

* * *

# 8th July

This is what the Lord Almighty says: 'These people say: "The time has not yet come for the

Lord's house to be built!" Then the word of the Lord came through the prophet Haggai: Is it a time for you yourselves to be living in your panelled houses, while this house remains a ruin? Now this is what the Lord Almighty says: Give careful thought to your ways. You have planted much, but harvested little. You eat, but never have enough. You drink, but never have your fill. You put on clothes, but are not warm. You earn wages, only to put them in a purse with holes in it.' This is what the Lord Almighty says: 'Give careful thought to your ways. Go up into the mountains and bring down timber and build the house, so that I may take pleasure in it and be honoured,' says the Lord.

Haggai 1:2–9

* * *

# 9th July

Jesus crossed to the far shore of the Sea of Galilee (that is, the Sea of Tiberias), and a great crowd followed him . . .

John 6:1

*O Jesus,*
*Be the canoe that holds me up in the sea of life;*
*Be the rudder that keeps me in the straight road;*
*Be the outrigger that supports me in times of great temptation.*
*Let Your Spirit be my sail that carries me through each day.*
*Keep my body strong, so I can paddle steadfastly*
*on in the voyage of life. Amen*

*A Prayer from Melanesian Islands*

The sea is so much part of our life; it surrounds our continents and islands, provides food, leisure, and employment for traders, seamen, ferries . . . there is always activity, challenge and danger. Lord, look on all Your people on the sea today – bless them and me on the sea of my life.

* * *

# 10th July

They went to a place called Gethsemane, and Jesus said to His disciples, 'Sit here while I pray'.

Mark 14:32

Prayer is an activity in the Spirit. It is our response through the Holy Spirit to the Father who in Jesus Christ has addressed each one of us by name and opened our ears to hear. In a sense, everything that I am and do is some sort of response to that address; but when I bow in prayer and say: O God . . . it is the supreme and clearest response, simply because praying can be given no other explanation that makes sense.

Rev. William W. Watty
West Indies

*Prayer is the Christian's vital breath . . .*
*O Thou by whom we come to God,*
*The life, the truth, the way,*
*The path or prayer Thyself hast trod:*
*Lord, teach us how to pray!*

*James Montgomery*

* * *

# 11th July

The moon marks off the seasons, and the sun knows when to go down. . . . How many are Your works, O Lord!.

Psalm 104:19–24

What an amazing system it is of which you and I are the product and that has sent this world and all the universe spinning along the grooves of time! If you were wandering through a meadow and picked up a watch and looked at its works, would you think that it had come together like that by accident? That it never had a Maker? It seems to me to be far more difficult to think that those marvellous laws rule the mighty forces in Nature without a creative intelligent mind and spirit behind them. I find that I have to go on and believe in a Creator by whose law the sun rises and sets. When I come to that conclusion, a new and shining meaning radiates from the most tremendous statement that language can speak, 'I believe in God'.

Basil Mathews

*The cold wind in the winter*
*The pleasant summer sun –*
*The ripe fruits in the garden*
*He made them every one!*

*C. F. Alexander*

* * *

# 12th July

The God of Peace be with you all.

Romans 15:33

*Like the hills serene and even,*
*Like the coursing clouds of heaven,*
*Like the heart that's been forgiven*
*Is the perfect peace of God.*

*Like the summer breezes playing,*
*Like the tall trees softly swaying,*
*Like the lips of silent praying*
*Is the perfect peace of God.*

*Like the morning sun ascended,*
*Like the scents of evening blended,*
*Like a friendship never ended*
*Is the perfect peace of God.*

*Michael Perry*

*Hold on to the good. Avoid every kind of evil. May God Himself, the God of Peace, sanctify you through and through. May your whole spirit, soul and body be kept blameless at the coming of our Lord Jesus Christ.*

*1 Thessalonians 5:21–23*

* * *

# 13th July

Jesus said: 'I am going to prepare a place for you. And if I go and prepare a place for you I will come back and take you to be with me. . . .'

John 14:3

*Lord, we know our own names:*
*Labelled, passported, well documented:*
*We know who we are and where we are going.*
*But we are still anxious, restless,*
*Constantly checking our labels:*
*Do we know who we are and where we are going?*
*You do not label us, but call us by name,*
*Love us, and hold our lives in Your hand:*
*Help us to know we are loved*
*And to trust in You as we go.*

Lord, I pray for all who are travelling today – by air, by road train or sea . . . for those travelling to new homes, to new lives . . . those who are travelling along life's road and those who today will travel to be with You . . . in all our comings and goings I know You are waiting and prepared.

* * *

# 14th July

Jesus asked: 'Which of these three do you think was a neighbour to the man who fell into the hands of robbers.'

Luke 10:36

An Aboriginal person was going down the road from birth to death in Australia. He fell among good-hearted people who gave him grog, sugar, tobacco, the Gospel – and took his land.

They left him by the edge of the town, the desert, the mining camp, disheartened, dispossessed and dying. A church warden came by that way and thought – 'They share with each other too much. We spend lots of money on them' . . . and she passed by in the other Australia.

A parish priest came and looked and thought, 'We should pray for them on Sunday. Sitting with them would be political and unacceptable to the congregation'. And he passed by in his liturgical correctness. Another Christian came that way. She got off her stereotype and out of her preconception. Sitting down she listened and heard the wounds and the treatment. She poured in the oil of identification and support.

Fred Wandmaker

*Lord, when You ask who is willing to be a neighbour, may I answer, 'Yes, Lord, I'm willing'.*

* * *

# 15th July

David praised the Lord in the presence of the whole assembly saying, Praise be to You, O Lord, God of our Father Israel, from everlasting to everlasting. Yours, O Lord is the greatness and the power and the glory and the majesty and the splendour, for everything in heaven and earth is Yours. Yours, O Lord is the kingdom; You are exalted as Head over all.

But who am I, and who are my people, that we should be able to give as generously as this? Everything comes from You, and we have given You only what comes from Your hands.

Then David said to the whole assembly: 'Praise the Lord Your God!'
So they all praised the Lord.

1 Chronicles 29:10–12, 14 and 20.

* * *

# 16th July

But the fruit of the Spirit is love, joy, peace, patience, kindness, goodness, faithfulness, gentleness and self-control.

Galatians 5:22

Tranquillity, gentleness and strength, carrying us through the changes of weather, the ups and downs of the route, the varied surface of the road; the inequalities of family life, emotional and professional disappointments, the sudden intervention of bad fortune or bad health, the rising and falling of our religious temperature. This is the threefold imprint of the Spirit on the soul surrendered to His great action.

Evelyn Underhill

*Lord of gentleness, Lord of all calm,*
*Whose voice is contentment, whose presence is balm;*
*Be there at our sleeping and give us we pray,*
*Your peace in our hearts, Lord, at the end of the day.*

*Jan Struther*

* * *

# 17th July

Be kind and compassionate to one another, forgiving each other just as in Christ God forgave you.

Ephesians 4:32

Have you ever noticed how much of Christ's life was spent in doing kind things, in merely doing kind things? Run over it with that in view and you will find that He spent a great proportion of His time simply in making people happy – in doing good turns to people. There is only one thing greater than happiness in the world, and that is, holiness; and that is not in our keeping; but God has put in our power the happiness of those about us, and that is largely to be secured by being kind to them.

Henry Drummond

*Jesus' hands were kind hands, doing good to all . . .*
*Take my hands, Lord Jesus, let them work for You;*
*Make them strong and gentle, kind in all I do.*

*Margaret Cropper*

* * *

# 18th July

You will again have compassion on us: you will tread our sins underfoot and hurl all our iniquities into the depth of the sea.

Micah 7:19

There is something merciless about the sea – so much of it and so constant. The depths of the sea must have seemed as good and as inaccessible a place as any to receive the iniquities of mankind, to the Old Testament prophets. . . .

Today, the sea still holds mystery and danger. I stare out at a timeless sea and try to grasp the timeless truth that God will take away all my hot temper, all my hurtful thoughts, all the mess that I know is inside my heart. . . . Lord, take my sinful self and loose all things hateful to You.

*Depth of mercy!*
*Can there be mercy still reserved for me? . . .*

*Charles Wesley*

* * *

# 19th July

On the Sabbath we went outside the city gate to the river, where we expected to find a place of prayer.

Acts 16:13

There is something inducive to prayer about a river – a calm, continuous motion . . . an ideal place for the apostles to go. But then, when we think of the way rivers were used in those days, we come to understand that not only were they places of contemplation, but also places where the washing was done, the children were washed, the cattle brought to drink, and so on and so forth! So perhaps we don't always need 'quiet' for talking to God – we ought to try it in the day-to-day routine chores, transport, shopping. . . . Lord help me to find You in any and every situation.

*Yes, we'll gather at the river*
*The beautiful, the beautiful river*
*Gather with the saints at the river*
*That flows by the throne of God.*

*Rev. R. Lowry*

* * *

# 20th July

Jesus said to Zacchaeus, 'Today salvation has come to this house . . .'

Luke 19:9

Many non-Aryan Christians owe their escape from Nazi Germany to a certain Quaker group based in London in the 1930s. The fear and desperation they must have endured is hard to imagine today – through the bravery and concern of the Quakers, they were able to re-establish their families in another country . . . their faith living proof that wherever in the world Christians may find themselves, they are united in a greater family. One of the young women who worked with the Quaker group was an Australian Honor Mary Young, and after the Second World War, she returned with her husband and family to Australia. Her best known translation is of a German hymn by Karl Spitta first published in 1833. Honor brought the sentiments of Christian home into today's language – truth which spans the centuries as well as the world!

*Happy the home that welcomes you Lord Jesus*
*Truest of friends,*
*Most honoured guest of all –*

*Honor M. Thwaites*

* * *

# 21st July

Praise the Lord, O my soul, all my inmost being praise His holy name.

Psalm 103:1

Dear Lord and God! O Holy One, O Lover of my soul! When you come to my heart, all that is within me will leap for joy. You are my hope and my refuge in my hour of peril. Yet I am still weak in love, imperfect in goodness, and I need your strength and comfort . . . free me from evil passions, and cure my heart of all its undisciplined emotions: then I shall be healthy and clean within, made fit for loving, strong for suffering, steadfast for enduring.

Thomas à Kempis
15th Century

*Jesu, Lover of my soul*
*Let me to Thy bosom fly. . . .*

*Charles Wesley*

* * *

# 22nd July

They fell down on their faces before the throne and worshipped God, saying: 'Amen! Praise and glory and wisdom and thanks and honour and power and strength be to our God for ever and ever. Amen!'

Then one of the elders asked me, 'These in white robes, who are they and where did they come from?'

I answered, 'Sir, you know.'

And he said, 'They are they who have come out of the great tribulation; they have washed their robes and made them white in the blood of the Lamb. Therefore, they are before the throne of God and serve Him day and night in His temple; and He who sits on the throne will spread His tent over them. Never again will they hunger; never again will they thirst. The sun will not beat upon them, nor any scorching heat. For the Lamb at the centre of the throne will be their shepherd; He will lead them to springs of living water. And God will wipe away every tear from their eyes.

Revelation 7:12–17

* * *

# 23rd July

It is good to wait quietly for the salvation of the Lord.

Lamentations 3:26

Switzerland, my present homeland, is a dream world where the wonders of God's creation are multiplied a thousandfold. . . . This past winter was unusually long, and spring seemed slow in coming. It was nearly May, and we were still waiting for the sun to break through the clouds so that we could bask in its warmth. We read in the Bible that all creation is also waiting – waiting to be set free from the weight of sin. Just as in nature the sun eventually breaks through the darkest of clouds, so in life Jesus can lift the clouds that darken our hearts.

Zsuzsanna Szegedi-Palvin

*Sorrow and sin may beset me about*
*Nothing can darken my brow!*
*Battling in faith I can joyfully shout*
*Jesus saves me now!*

*Anon*

* * *

# 24th July

And Jesus took the children in His arms, put His hands on them and blessed them

Mark 10:16

We tend to look at the writers of Victorian hymns for children as being too poetic for the minds of this century. However, the life of one such writer would make a good television serial. Walter John Mathams was born in London, went to sea as a young man and got gold-rush fever, joining the fortune-seeking thousands in Alaska. After Alaska, Walter Mathams entered the Baptist ministry, suffered some bad health and went to Australia to recover. From 1902–05 he served as a much-loved Chaplain to the Forces in Egypt! He concluded his ministry in the Church of Scotland ministering in the islands. A man of action! Not the stereotype nineteenth century poet – Lord, I thank and praise You for the exciting lives of Your servants who, out of their experiences and faith, speak through their words for me today.

*Jesus, Friend of little children*
*Be a Friend to me:*
*Take my hand and ever lead me*
*Close to Thee.*

*Walter J. Mathams*

* * *

# 25th July

And we pray this in order that you may live a life worthy of the Lord and may please Him in every way, bearing fruit in every good work.

Colossians 1:10

Let the Church remember this: that every maker and worker is called to serve God in his profession or trade – not outside it. The official Church wastes time and energy in demanding that secular workers should neglect their proper vocation in order to do Christian work – by which she means ecclesiastical work. The only Christian work is good work well done. . . . then all work will be Christian work, whether it is Church embroidery, or sewage-farming.

Dorothy Sayers.

*If you want to produce Christian work, be a Christian, and try to make a work of beauty into which you have put your heart; do not adopt a Christian pose.*

*Jacques Maritain*

* * *

# 26th July

Awake, my soul! Awake, harp and lyre! I will awaken the dawn.

Psalm 57:9

The real problem of the Christian life comes where people do not usually look for it. It comes the very moment you wake up each morning. All your wishes and hopes for the day rush at you like wild animals. And the first job each morning consists simply in shoving them all back, in listening to that other voice, taking the other point of view, letting that other larger, stronger, quieter life come flowing in. And so on, all day . . . we can only do it for moments at first, letting Him work at the right part of us. It is the difference between paint on the surface and a dye which soaks right through.

C. S. Lewis

*Awake, my soul, and with the sun*
*Thy daily stage of duty run;*
*Shake off dull sloth, and joyful rise*
*To pay thy morning sacrifice.*

*Thomas Ken*

* * *

# 27th July

Repent and do the things you did at first.

Revelation 2:5

What a very unfashionable word 'repent' has become! There seems to be a constant striving to be right all the time and a total inability to admit error. We have lost the art of being sorry let alone saying that we are sorry. The people who are found within the pages of the Bible leap at us with a realism and contemporary flavour for the very reason that they too found it so hard to 'repent'. The prophets main message was 'repent' – John the Baptist cried, 'Repent', and our Lord Jesus said, 'unless you repent . . .' Dear Lord, why is my heart so proud? How can you work the miracle of salvation in me? I long to start again to be genuinely sorry and return to the cross of Jesus.

*God creates out of nothing. Wonderful you say. Yes, to be sure, but He does what is still more wonderful: He makes saints out of sinners!*

*Soren Kierkegaard*

* * *

# 28th July

To him who sits of the throne and to the Lamb be praise and honour and glory and power for ever and ever!

Revelation 5:13

The famous musician and composer Bach was an intensely devout man. 'His great religious masterpieces were the natural outpourings of his inmost soul. In the *Little Chronicle* is written, "Deep down in his great heart he always carried his Lord Crucified, and his noblest music is his secret cry for a clearer vision of the risen Christ. In his lullaby in the *Christmas Cantata* he could write music tender enough for the Babe of Bethlehem; in the Crucifixion of his *Great Mass* he could find strains grand enough for the Saviour of Calvary. At the end of his earlier scores he always inscribed the letters; S.D.G. – To God be the Glory!'

F. W. Boreham

*O come to the Father, through Jesus the Son:*
*And give Him the glory! Great things He hath done!*

*Frances Jane van Alstyne*

* * *

# 29th July

And the word of the Lord came to him: 'What are you doing here Elijah?'

He replied, 'I have been very zealous for the Lord God Almighty. The Israelites have rejected your covenant, broken down your altars, and put your prophets to death with the sword. I am the only one left, and now they are trying to kill me too.'

The Lord said: 'Go out and stand on the mountain in the presence of the Lord, for the Lord is about the pass by.'

Then a great and powerful wind tore the mountains apart and shattered the rocks before the Lord, but the Lord was not in the wind. After the wind there was an earthquake, but the Lord was not in the earthquake. After the earthquake came a fire, but the Lord was not in the fire. And after the fire came a gentle whisper. When Elijah heard it, he pulled his cloak over his face and went out and stood at the mouth of the cave. Then a voice said to him: 'What are you doing here, Elijah?'

1 Kings 19:9–14

* * *

# 30th July

Day and night they never stopped saying: 'Holy, holy, holy is the Lord God Almighty, who was, and is, and is to come.'

Revelation 4:8

For many centuries there had been no such thing as hymns: the psalms were the only form of musical worship apart from chants. Then came the inovators, the pioneers of singing in church, Isaac Watts, Tate and Brady, John Newton, William Cowper and, notably, Charles Wesley. Following in their footsteps Reginald Heber wrote his hymns specifically to integrate them with liturgy of the

Church Year. He was a hard-working man of greatest promise who died suddenly whilst swimming. When he died he was only 43 yet he had been Bishop of Calcutta for three years and was highly respected and loved. His best known hymn reminds many of their school days:

*Holy, holy, holy, Lord God Almighty!*
*Early in the morning our song shall rise to Thee:*
*Holy, holy, holy, merciful and mighty,*
*God in three Persons, Blessed Trinity!*

*Reginald Heber*

* * *

# 31st July

Jesus said: 'Whoever wants to be first must be slave of all. For even the Son of Man did not come to be served but to serve. . . .'

Mark 10:44

Christianity has no respect for the labels which the world attaches to a man. The world places a man according to the size of his bank account, the number of people he controls, his prestige in whatever field his work may happen to lie. Christianity rates a man by the service that he renders to his fellow men. The result is that the man whom the world accounts great may well be worthless in the Kingdom of God; while the man who appears of no standing in the world may well be the greatest. The test in the Kingdom of God is the test of service.

Dr William Barclay

*He has scattered those who are proud*
*in their inmost thoughts –*
*He has brought down rulers from their thrones,*
*But has lifted up the humble . . .*

*Mary's song: Luke 1:51 & 52*

* * *

# 1st August

Dear Friends, now we are children of God.

1 John: 3:2

Lord, help me to use my trials, my needs, my failures, my successes, my gifts, perhaps especially my suffering, not to measure myself, but to understand – to love, to be able to share in the same struggles that those around me are living through. For the people on this beach are not distantly related to me – we are all brothers and sisters . . . brown, black, blonde, pink, our only purpose is to learn to live in love as children of God.

Frank Topping

*Children of the King are we*
*May we loyal to Him be;*
*Try to please Him every day*
*In our work and in our play –*
*Then we truthfully can sing:*
*We are children of the King!*

*Whitfield G. Wills*

* * *

# 2nd August

Jesus said: 'A time is coming and has now come when the true worshippers will worship the Father in spirit and truth, for they are the kind of worshippers the Father seeks.'

John 4:23

But the Lord showed me, so that I did see clearly, that He did not dwell in these temples which men had commanded and set up, but in people's hearts; for both Stephen and the Apostle Paul bore testimony that He did not dwell in temples made with hands, not even in that which He had once commanded to be built, since He put an end to it;

but that His people were His temple and He dwelt in them. This opened to me as I walked in the fields . . .

George Fox

*You alone are my strength, my shield,*
*To You alone may my spirit yield;*
*You alone are my heart's desire*
*And I long to worship You.*

*Martin Nystrom*

* * *

# 3rd August

Anna gave thanks to God and spoke about the child to all who were looking forward to the redemption of Jerusalem.

Luke 2:38

At any time it is obvious how much pleasure older people gain from the company of a small child. And Anna, the old lady who during her long years of widowhood had devoted herself entirely to prayer, fasting and worship in the temple, was thrilled to meet Mary and Joseph with the young Jesus. To Anna was given special insight that He was indeed the Messiah and we can look on Anna as the first missionary for we read that she lost no time in telling everyone around about the child. I'm sure many – possibly most – dismissed her talk in the patronising way we often treat elderly widows. Lord, forgive me for my attitudes and impatience towards age. I pray for Anna's purity and purpose, for her delight in the Christ child and her uninhibited tongue.

*Though an infant now we view Him,*
*He shall fill his Father's throne;*
*Gather all the nations to Him*
*Every knee shall then bow down:*

*James Montgomery*

* * *

# 4th August

But mark this: . . . people will be lovers of themselves, lovers of money . . . ungrateful, unholy . . . conceited lovers of pleasure rather than lovers of God – having a form of godliness but denying its power.

2 Timothy 3:1–4

'Things are seldom what they seem' trills a song from Gilbert and Sullivan's *H.M.S. Pinafore*. Very true! A glance at the newspaper in the property market or the used-car section and we know all too well how cleverly appearances can deceive. It is very easy to become deceived spiritually if we put all our confidence in second, third, or even fourth-hand faith. There is only one way to God and that is through Jesus Christ His Son . . . nobody else can arrange this experience for us, we cannot do it by letter or telephone . . . we cannot leave it till next year or next day. Lord, open my eyes to my own self-deception . . . give me that new heart that affirms Your holy power.

*Spirit of God within me, possess my human frame. . . .*
*Strive till that image Adam lost,*
*New-minted and restored,*
*In shining splendour brightly bears*
*The likeness of the Lord.*

*Timothy Dudley-Smith*

* * *

# 5th August

This is what the Sovereign Lord showed me: a basket of ripe fruit.

'What do you see, Amos?' He asked.

'A basket of ripe fruit,' I answered.

Then the Lord said to me, 'The time is ripe for my people Israel; I will spare them no longer. In that day,' declares the Sovereign Lord, 'the songs in the temple will turn to wailing. Many, many bodies – flung everywhere! Silence!'

Hear this, you who trample the needy and do away with the poor of the land, saying, 'When will the New Moon be over that we may sell grain, and the Sabbath be ended that we may market wheat?' skimping the measure, boosting the price and cheating with dishonest scales, buying the poor with silver and the needy for a pair of sandals, selling even the sweepings with the wheat.

The Lord has sworn by the pride of Jacob: 'I will never forget anything they have done . . . I will send a famine through the land – not a famine of food or a thirst for water, but a famine of hearing the words of the Lord.'

Amos 8:1–7 & 11

* * *

# 6th August

And Jesus took the children in his arms, put His hands on them and blessed them.

Mark 10:16

When I muttered, 'Forgive them', I wondered how far I was being dramatic, and if I really meant it; because I looked at their faces as they stood round, taking it in turn to flog me, and their faces were hard and cruel, and some of them were evidently enjoying their cruelty. But, by the Grace of God, I saw these men not as they were, but as they had been. Once they were little children, with their brothers and their sisters – happy in their parents' love, in those far-off days before they had been conditioned by their false nationalistic ideals. And it is hard to hate little children.

Bishop John Leonard Wilson

*Lord Christ, yourself a child*
*Within an earthly home,*
*Our children bless in every place,*
*That they may all behold your face,*
*And, knowing you, may grow in grace.*

*F. Bland Tucker*

* * *

# 7th August

On the third day a wedding took place at Cana in Galilee. Jesus' mother was there, and Jesus and his disciples had also been invited to the wedding.

John 2:1

God is guiding your marriage. Marriage is more than your love for each other. It has a higher dignity and power for it is God's holy ordinance. . . . In your love you see your two selves as solitary figures in the world; in marriage you see yourselves as links in the chain of the generations. . . . In your love you see only the heaven of your bliss, through marriage you are placed at a post of responsibility towards the world and to mankind. It is not your love which sustains the marriage, but from now on the marriage that sustains your love.

Deitrich Bonhoeffer

*Lord, you know the difficulties in every marriage – but thank You for the precious closeness that love brings . . . the joy of being together every day. Give us a fresh awareness of each other's needs and renewed contentment in marriage.*

* * *

# 8th August

They will spread out their hands as a swimmer spreads out his hands to swim.

Isaiah 25:11

Donald Soper was taught to swim by his grandfather who told the small Donald, 'If you'll only do the things that the expert swimmers have proved to be right, you'll find the water will hold you up. I'll be beside you if anything goes wrong.'

In later years Donald Soper found the parallel to faith in his experience of learning to swim: 'Now what's true about learning to swim properly is true about learning to live properly. Jesus said that God made this world in such a way that if we do the right things – the good, true honourable, decent, straight-forward things – we shall find that they will work . . . and He says to us all "I'll be beside you if anything goes wrong" '.

*Finally brothers, whatever is true, whatever is noble, whatever is right, whatever is pure, whatever is admirable – think about such things – and the God of peace be with you.*

*Philippians 4:8*

* * *

# 9th August

Peter said: 'We are witnesses of everything Jesus did in the country of the Jews and in Jerusalem.'

Acts 10:39

The fire of truth in Peter's preaching brought thousands into the early church. His speech was so powerful because he was a living witness of his Lord, so that he knew what he was talking about. And so still, the people of deep faith can inspire others because of the experience which shines through, and we can look at certain people and know beyond a shadow of doubt that they know what they are talking about. Lord, I need to hear Your witnesses to help me emerge from my shadows . . . to feel that I can cope after all with Your strength.

*'I determined to retire for a short time into Germany . . . I hoped the conversing with those holy men who were themselves living witnesses of the full power of faith, would be a means, under God, of so establishing my soul, that I might go on from faith to faith and from strength to strength.'*

*From John Wesley's Journal, 7 July, 1783*

* * *

# 10th August

He will not let your foot slip – he who watches over you . . . will neither slumber nor sleep.

Psalm 121:3–4

To withhold sleep is a tried and tested form of torture. To toss and turn at night chewing over our problems a form of self-inflicted torture . . . no amount of lost sleep will help. Lord, why do I do this to myself – why can't I learn to bring everything to You in prayer, to lay down my burden and ask You only to hold me through the night. Perhaps it's really that I am not so certain that You can care for my personal needs – but, of course, how can I understand Almighty God? Help me to trust – and to sleep . . .

*Have courage for the great sorrows of life and patience for the small ones. And when you have laboriously accomplished your daily task go to sleep. God is awake.*

*Victor Hugo*

* * *

# 11th August

Then he sent some more servants to those who had been invited to the banquet to tell them to come, but they refused to come.

Matthew 22:3

Lord Jesus Christ, we love to celebrate the joy of weddings birthdays and success. . . . To meet around a table and share food and news, To give and receive presents. You said: 'The Kingdom of God is like that! The Kingdom of God is among us . . . here and now. People of every race and age group are set free by Your cross, Forgiven – liberated from selfishness – prejudice and insularity.

People from every part of the world are released from all that divides and separates, to form a new community,

enjoying one another's company, listening to and receiving from one another at the great feast God has prepared.
Teach us to make time to go on building up relationships with others who are invited to celebrate God's feast.

Maureen Edwards

*In memory of the Saviour's love*
*We keep the sacred feast*
*Where every humble, contrite heart*
*Is made a welcome guest.*

*Thomas Cotterill*

* * *

# 12th August

The time is coming, declares the Lord, 'when I will make a new covenant with the house of Israel and with the house of Judah. It will not be like the covenant I made with their forefathers when I took them by the hand to lead them out of Egypt, because they broke my covenant. . . .
This is the covenant that I will make with the house of Israel: I will put my law in their minds and write it on their hearts. I will be their God and they will be my people. No longer will a man teach his neighbour or a man his brother saying, "Know the Lord", because they will all know me, from the least of them to the greatest,' declares the Lord. 'For I will forgive their wickedness and will remember their sins no more.'

Jeremiah 31:31–34

* * *

# 13th August

What is man that You are mindful of him? . . .
You made him a little lower than the angels . . .
and put everything under his feet.

Hebrews 2:6–7 and 8

Take 10 gallons of water, enough fat for 7 barrels of soap, carbon for 9,000 pencils, enough phosphorous to make 2,200 matches, sufficient iron for a single nail, just enough lime to whitewash a chicken coup, plus small quantities of magnesium and sulphur and you have – the human being. Or that is supposed to be our chemical make-up. But God has made us more than a hotch-potch of chemicals – he has given us a soul . . . the sacredness of personality . . . the capacity to learn and to love. God has made us 'a little lower than the angels' . . . we don't merely exist to be counted – each soul counts to Him.

Jake Watson

*Angels holy, high and lowly*
*Sing the praises of the Lord!*
*Earth and sky; all living nature*
*Man, the stamp of Thy Creator*
*Praise of Praise we Christ our Lord.*

*based on John S. Blackie*

* * *

# 14th August

When Jesus took the bread, gave thanks, broke it and began to give it to them, their eyes were opened and they recognised Him.

Luke 24:30

During the war, as serviceman landed on one of the islands in the Philippines, he saw a starving little girl and offered her a bite of his sandwich. Her mind had been so affected by propaganda that she refused it – it might be poisoned. The serviceman took a bite of the sandwich and said to her, 'I take a bite – you take a bite.' She relaxed and finished the sandwich. In Jesus, and I say this most reverently, we find God doing much the same thing. He says, 'I take a bite – you take a bite.' You see, Jesus not only tasted death for every man, He tasted Life with every man. He asks us to do nothing that He Himself would not do.

Selwyn Hughes

*O Thou who this mysterious bread*
*Didst in Emmaus break,*
*Return, herewith our souls to feed,*
*And to Thy followers speak.*

*Charles Wesley*

* * *

# 15th August

A furious squall came up, and the waves broke over the boat so that it was nearly swamped.

Mark 4:37

Even with modern, sophisticated radio, radar and methods of weather forecasting, the sea remains untameable and unpredictable. Boats are all too easily swamped and lives in danger . . . every year we read of accidents and tragedies at sea and on beaches when people have been caught unawares by 'freak' conditions. The Christian life is similarly unpredictable and open to danger. We need always to be alert and to accept that conditions can change rapidly and unbelievably – a marriage into a divorce, a healthy teenager into a drug addict, a caring parent into a geriatric shell. O Lord whose power never changes, whose love never ends, hold me in my furious squalls . . . with Christ beside me I shall not be swamped.

*On a wild and stormy ocean*
*Sinking 'neath the wave,*
*Souls that perish, heed the message*
*Christ has come to save!*

*E. Nathan*

* * *

# 16th August

Jesus said: 'For I have come down from Heaven not to do my will, but to do the will of Him who sent me.'

John 6:38

'To accept the Will of God never leads to the miserable feeling that it is useless to strive any more. God does not ask for the dull, weak, sleepy acquiescence of indolence. He asks for something vivid and strong. He asked us to co-operate with Him, actively willing what He wills, our only aim His glory.' So wrote Amy Carmichael.

I need encouragement today, Lord, I need to be reminded that Jesus lived faithfully to Your will facing everything, even death for Your glory – and here am I bogged down and feeling 'what's the point?' Lift my eyes to Heaven and give me Your strength to carry on doing Your will.

*Take my will and make it thine*
*It shall be no longer mine;*
*Take my heart, it is thine own,*
*It shall be thy royal throne.*

*Frances Ridley Havergal*

* * *

# 17th August

Therefore, if anyone is in Christ, he is a new creation; the old has gone and the new has come! All this is from God who reconciled us to Himself through Christ –

2 Corinthians 5:17

Lord, I'm thinking today of those who share in the ministry of reconciliation . . . probation officers and youth workers, social workers and chaplains in hospitals and prisons. I pray for young lives which long to be new creations but leap from school to unemployment, from home to friendless bed-sits . . . for those who seek to give those lives purpose. I think of all who harbour resentments and grudges which prevent their lives being made new – may we find the liberating joy of finding reconciliation to one another and to You.

*Lord Jesus Christ, give us power and courage to carry on Your work of reconciling love that men and women might repent of their sins and turn to You. . . .*

*Prayer from the Christian Council of Asia, 1987*

* * *

# 18th August

The Lord protects the simple-hearted; when I was in great need, He saved me.

Psalm 116:6

A gentle, simple man spent a fortnight at the interdenominational Corrymeela Centre in Northern Ireland. When he got back home again he was overwhelmed by his holiday and kept repeating to everyone how wonderful it had been. 'What was so good?' asked his minister. 'Was it the weather? The food? The activities?' No, it was none of those – what had been so wonderful was that in the entire two weeks no one had laughed at him. He had been accepted, had been listened to and been loved for the person he was, and it had given him new heart.

*Lord, I'm guilty of tipping the grin at those who don't grasp things as quickly as I do – I'm guilty of impatience – of intolerance – and yet I have so much to learn. Teach me how to understand, to protect and to cherish all Your children.*

* * *

# 19th August

For this is what the Sovereign Lord says: I myself will search for my sheep and look after them. As a shepherd looks after his scattered flock when he is with them, so will I look after my sheep. . . . I will tend them in a good pasture, and the mountain heights of Israel will be their grazing land. . . . I myself will tend my sheep, and make them lie down, declares the Sovereign Lord. I will search for the lost and bring back the strays. I will bind up the injured and strengthen the weak, but the sleek and the strong I will destroy. I will shepherd the flock with justice. . . . I the Lord will be their God – I the Lord have spoken.

Ezekiel 34:11–12, 14–16, 24

* * *

# 20th August

Jesus said: 'When you pray, go into your room, close the door, and pray to your Father, who is unseen.'

Matthew 6:6

As to how we should pray for others, I find it a help myself to go in my imagination to them where they are, to Africa, or to a hospital, or to their room, or to some place where we have been together, and to kneel there with them beside me, and so to say my prayer for them. . . . We may pray for them as we will, but I would have you turn again and again to the 'Our Father'. . . . And sometimes leave all words, and simply kneel there and hold them up, as it were, one by one in your arms to show them to God, as when once He walked among men in Palestine they brought young children to Him for Him to bless them.

Bernard Clements

*Prayer is the burden of a sigh*
*The falling of a tear:*
*The upward glancing of an eye*
*When none but God is near.*

*James Montgomery*

* * *

# 21st August

As Jesus walked beside the Sea of Galilee, he saw Simon and his brother Andrew casting a net into the lake, for they were fishermen. 'Come, follow me!' said Jesus.

Mark 1:16

Our Lord says to us, 'Follow me'. He does not say, 'Settle down with me'. We are pilgrims, travellers, adventurers, and all the while we must be travelling on. We travel on in every way, in our thoughts, in our lives, in our sense of spiritual things, in our ideals of holiness. We shall always be travelling on to what is greater and more beautiful, so that we may be perfect, as our Father in Heaven is perfect.

Father Andrew

*Give me courage when the world is rough,*
*Keep me loving though the world is tough;*
*Leap and sing in all I do,*
*Keep me travelling along with You:*

*Sydney Carter*

* * *

# 22nd August

On each side of the river stood the tree of life.

Revelation 22:2

We pray for the victims of war and for those who profit by war – the nations who produce and sell ever more sophisticated weapons: we pray for those who use them to fight and kill. Forgive them for their trade in human blood. Show them a better way of living, make them and us more sensitive to each other, more aware of Your image in each human being. We put our trust in You. We need Your tree of life to heal our suffering, to feed every nation with Your fruits of justice, love and peace. May Your kingdom come in our lives.

A student from Mozambique

*Peace is flowing like a river . . . flowing out through you and me –*
*Spreading out in to the desert . . . setting all the captives free.*

* * *

# 23rd August

Come and listen, all you who fear God: let me tell you what He has done for me.

Psalm 66:16

There is no difficulty in recounting to friends and neighbours the events of a recent holiday or the deeds of kindness shown to us at times of need – there is always an abundance of tales remembered where a person has been deceived or robbed. We are all-seeing – all knowing – all passing-it-on except in relation to what God has been doing in our lives. Today, I suggest that if you cannot see what God has done for you, then ask yourself, 'What have I done for Him?'

*Live for self – you live in vain:*
*Live for Christ – you live again.*
*Pass it on! Pass it on!*

*Henry Burton*

* * *

# 24th August

I can do everything through Him who gives me strength.

Philippians 4:13

Never again will I confess, 'I can't' for 'I can do all things through Christ who strengtheneth me.' Never again will I confess fear, for 'God hath not given me a spirit of fear, but of power, and of love and of a sound mind.' Never again will I confess weakness for 'The Lord is the strength of my life.' Never again will I confess worries and frustrations, for I am 'Casting all my cares upon Him who careth for me.' In Christ I am care-free!

Don Gossett
(New Zealand)

*Are we weak and heavy laden*
*Cumbered with a load of care?*
*Precious Jesus still our refuge*
*Take it to the Lord in prayer.*

*Joseph Scriven*

* * *

# 25th August

Jacob set up a stone pillar at the place where God had talked to him. . . . Jacob named the place where God had talked with him Bethel.

Genesis 35:14

A fellow internee with Eric Liddell gave her explanation of his 'secret', the reason for his charisma: 'My husband was in his dormitory and shared the secret with him. Every morning about 6 a.m. with curtains tightly drawn to keep in the shining of the peanut oil lamp lest the prowling sentries would think someone was trying to escape, Eric used to climb out of his top bunk, then, at a small Chinese table, the two men would sit together with their Bibles and notebooks. Silently they read, prayed, thought about the day's duties, noted what should be done. Eric talked to God all the time . . . naturally . . . his life was grounded in God, in faith and in trust.'

*Talk with us Lord, Thyself reveal . . .*
*Speak to our hearts and let us feel*
*The kindling of Thy love.*

*Charles Wesley*

* * *

# 26th August

Therefore, as God's chosen people, holy and dearly loved, clothe yourselves with compassion, kindness, humility, gentleness and patience. Bear with each other and forgive whatever grievances you may have against one another. Forgive as the Lord forgave you. And over all these virtues put on love, which binds them all together in perfect unity.

Let the peace of Christ rule in your hearts, since as members of one body you were called to peace. And be thankful. Let the word of Christ dwell in you richly as you teach and admonish one another with all wisdom, and as you sing psalms, hymns and spiritual songs with gratitude in your hearts to God. And whatever you do, whether in word or deed, do it all in the name of the Lord Jesus, giving thanks to God the Father through him.

Colossians 3:12–17

* * *

# 27th August

Grace and peace to you from God our Father and the Lord Jesus Christ.

2 Corinthians 1:2

*Grace – is God making sure that you get what you don't deserve.*
*Mercy – is God making sure that you don't get what you deserve.*
*Peace – is what you enjoy when you accept His grace and mercy!*

*Anon*

Such small words, grace, mercy and peace – words that can transform hell into heaven. Words that give the follower of Jesus Christ the assurance that His love surrounds our every move and our every breath. Three small words which make the day easier to face with real joy and thanksgiving in our hearts.

* * *

# 28th August

The Lord came and stood there as at the other times, calling: 'Samuel! Samuel!

1 Samuel 3:10

William Penn had his first experience of God at the early age of 11. It was 1656, and he was alone in his room when he felt surprised by an inner comfort and an external glory which filled the small room. From that time on he often said that he knew the seal of divinity and immortality and that there was a God who spoke directly to the souls of men and women. That assurance was to carry him through all the trials of life and faith in his celebrated life.

*The light comes, when it does come, rather suddenly and strangely . . . Sooner or later you will 'see', if only for a moment, but no one can anticipate that moment. It comes when one least expects it. It does not last, but the certainty it conveys does last.*

*Evelyn Underhill*

* * *

# 29th August

One day, Jesus was praying in a certain place. When He had finished one of His disciples said to Him, 'Lord, teach us how to pray'.

Luke 11:1

It's funny how we can pray all kinds of different prayers of thanks and penitence, traditional or modern, yet when there is something of tremendous importance tugging at our heart the words dry up. We just don't know how to start. The disciples had most probably prayed in the synagogue all their lives until, in the presence of their Master, they realised how inadequate they were. Lord God, what can I say? Where do I begin?

A prayer by Maurice Rowntree found in a notebook after his death:
*Father, I come to Thee, feeling my failure to live as Thou wouldst have me live, asking for cleansing and for the renewal within me of Thy life . . . Here is all that I have – my powers of body, mind and soul, my possessions, loves and affections – use all these gifts, I pray Thee, so that according to Thy will I may promote the coming of Thy Kingdom on earth.*

* * *

# 30th August

Evil men do not understand justice, but those who seek the Lord understand it fully.

Proverbs 28:5

If only people could naturally treat other people as they themselves would like to be treated. In theory, it sounds so simple, such common sense, yet our human nature bows to the evil influences around us, we are weak and block out our understanding of the Bible teaching. Lord, I'm too busy looking at the faults in others . . . too busy to seek Your will for me this day . . . in quietness I need to study Your word, to understand that my decisions must be based on fairness, underlined with tolerance, together with the awareness of my own inadequacy. Open my ears, Lord and my eyes as well as my mind.

*Most people are bothered by those passages of Scripture they don't understand – but I have always noticed that the passages that bother me are the ones I do understand.*

*Mark Twain*

* * *

# 31st August

My loved one had a vineyard on a fertile hillside . . . he looked for a crop of good grapes, but it yielded only bad fruit.

Isaiah 5:1–2

Every gardener or grower knows the disappointment of a bad crop – and anyone who has stored fruit knows the effect of one bad fruit. It is quite natural, then, for the parables in the Old Testament and the New to be directly concerned with things we all understand; and the parallel of fruit and people is obvious. Lord, I know that bad fruit in my life infects other parts, forgive the sour relationships, the bruised feelings, the smell of scandal, faith that has 'gone off' . . . give me the will-power to get rid of everything impure so that the witness of my life may yield only good fruit.

*Jesus said: Watch out for false prophets. They come in sheep's clothing, but inwardly they are ferocious wolves. By their fruit you will recognise them. . . . Every tree that does not bear good fruit is cut down and thrown into the fire.*

*Matthew 7:15–19*

* * *

# 1st September

Where, O death is your victory? Where, O death is your sting?

Hosea 13:14 & 1 Corinthians 15:55

God, in all His power and strength and comfort, is available to every one of us today. He was revealed to me not because I was a special person but because I was willing in faith to accept what God gave. I know what I say is true, not just because the Bible says so, or because the Church has told us, but because I have experienced it myself; I know that whether you are despondent or in joy, whether you are apathetic or full of enthusiasm, there is available for you – at this moment – the whole life of God, with its victory over sin and pain and death.

Bishop John Leonard Wilson

*The sting of death is sin, and the power of sin is the law.*
*But thanks be to God! He gives us the victory through our Lord Jesus Christ*

*1 Corinthians 15:56–57*

* * *

# 2nd September

Those who accepted his (Peter's) message, were baptised, and about three thousand were added to their number that day. They devoted themselves to the apostles' teaching and to the fellowship, to the breaking of bread and to prayer. Everyone was filled with awe, and many wonders and miraculous signs were done by the apostles. All the believers were together and had everything in common. Selling their possessions and goods, they gave to anyone as he had need. Every day they continued to meet together in the temple courts. They broke bread in their homes and ate together with glad and sincere hearts, praising God and enjoying the favour of all the people. And the Lord added to their number daily those who were being saved.

Acts 2:41–47

* * *

# 3rd September

For there is no difference between Jew and Gentile – the same Lord is Lord of all and richly blesses all who call on him . . .

Romans 10:12

The banner behind the three tall candles said: We are one in the Spirit. I looked around the small Hawaiian country church where the banner was hanging. The minister bringing God's word was Korean; the song leader, Hawaiian; the organist a Caucasian. The faces of the choir showed a lovely blending of Chinese, Hawaiian, Japanese, Samoan, Filipino and Korean. In the pew next to me sat a man from Tonga, and behind us were three young men from Fiji. I knew the banner was not a lie; all persons there were 'one in the Spirit'.

Rene Wade Ross (Hawaii)

*In Christ all races meet –*
*When Christ is throned as Lord,*
*All shall forsake their fear:*
*One Lord, in one great name unite us all.*

*G. W. Briggs*

* * *

# 4th September

He (the living God) has shown kindness by giving you rain from heaven and crops in their seasons; He provides you with plenty of food and fills your hearts with joy.

Acts 14:17

*We plough the fields*
*And scatter the good seed on the land,*
*But it is fed and watered*
*By God's Almighty hand;*
*He sends the snow in winter*
*The warmth to swell the grain,*
*The breezes and the sunshine*
*And soft, refreshing rain:*

*All good gifts around us*
*Are sent from heaven above*
*Then thank the Lord, O thank the Lord*
*For all His love.*

*M. Claudius*

You care for the land and water it; You enrich it abundantly. The streams of God are filled with water to provide the people with grain, for so You have ordained it . . . the meadows are covered with flocks and the valleys mantled with grain; they shout for joy and sing.

Psalm 65:9 and 11

* * *

# 5th September

The voice spoke to Peter a second time, 'Do not call anything impure that God has made clean.'

Acts 10:15

Peter had such a hard lesson to learn – in fact he had to change the attitude of a lifetime. What God has made we have no right to look at with upturned nose. Lord, what makes us take decisions on 'desirables' and 'undesirables'? We know the pain and humiliation caste systems cause, we know the evil of apartheid, and history is full of horrific events where racial hatred and religious intolerance became the ruling passion. Each human catastrophe begins in such disarmingly simple and small ways – I pray that I can be alert to small beginnings which may become disastrous influences later.

*The people on this beach*
*Are not distantly related to me –*
*We are all brothers and sisters,*
*Brown, black, blonde and pink.*
*Our only purpose is to learn to live in love as children of God.*

*Frank Topping*

* * *

# 6th September

Multitudes, multitudes in the valley of decision! For the day of the Lord is near in the valley of decision.

Joel 3:14

Decisions! Decisions! Big ones and little ones – they crop up all through our lives: which subjects to take at school, which polytechnic or university to choose, what kind of job, to have a holiday or a new car, deciding whether to stay or leave an unhappy marriage, does mother come to live with us or not. . . . Through life, I know I will make many wrong decisions and I ask, Lord, for Your grace to admit failure. I cannot regret decisions because to fight shy of making decisions is to renounce my responsibilities, to fudge issues and weaken my character. But the one decision I can never retract is the one made to follow Jesus Christ.

*I have decided to follow Jesus. . . .*
*No turning back – no turning back!*

*The world behind me – the cross before me. . . .*
*No turning back – no turning back!*

*Cliff Barrows and Don Hustad*

* * *

# 7th September

Before a word is on my tongue, You know it completely, O Lord.

Psalm 139:4

After a long, distinguished life, the American Quaker poet and journalist John Greenleaf Whittier died on 7 September 1892. Non-Quaker worship doesn't give much space to silence, sometimes it would seem we are afraid of silence in case we realise that God does actually know our innermost thoughts – our secret selves. Lord, I squirm with embarrassment for the light You shine into my thoughts. . . . I can only be overwhelmed to know that knowing me as You do, You still love me, forgive me and listen to my prayers. I bring You praise and honour and my heartfelt thanksgiving in the silence of these precious moments.

*Our thoughts lie open to the light*
*And naked to Thy glance.*
*Our secret sins are in the light*
*Of Thy pure countenance.*

*John Greenleaf Whittier*

* * *

# 8th September

The gift of God is eternal life in Christ Jesus our Lord.

Romans 7:23

*'What, giving again?'*
*I asked in dismay,*
*'And must I keep giving,*
*And giving always?'*
*'Oh no' said the angel,*
*Whose eyes pierced me through:*
*'Just stop when the Saviour*
*Stops giving to you!'*

*Anon*

And now He is giving his gifts to us all –
For no one is worthless and each one is called.

Graham Kendrick

* * *

# 9th September

Then Peter began to speak: 'I now realise how true it is that God does not show favouritism but accepts men from every nation who fear Him and do what is right. This is the message God sent to the people of Israel, telling the good news of peace through Jesus Christ who is Lord of all. You know what has happened throughout Judea, beginning in Galilee after the baptism that John preached – how God annointed Jesus of Nazareth with the Holy Spirit and power, and how He went around doing good and healing all who were under the power of the devil, because God was with Him. We are witnesses of everything He did in the country of the Jews and in Jerusalem. They killed Him by hanging Him on a tree, but God raised Him from the dead on the third day and caused Him to be seen. He was not seen by all the people but by witnesses whom God had already chosen – by us who ate and drank with Him after He rose from the dead.

Acts10:34–41

* * *

# 10th September

... suddenly a light from heaven flashed around him. He fell to the ground and heard a voice say to him: 'Saul, Saul, why do you persecute me?'

Acts 9:4

I wonder how much of my 'religion' is the accident of my upbringing? Perhaps we are all unconsciously arrogant in our belief that we have a monopoly of the truth, and it does us good to realise for the odd moment or two that God has other instruments of His truth, instruments which take us by surprise. Sadhu Sundar Singh was born in the Punjab into a strict Sikh family. He was diligently anti-Christian, even to the extent of tearing up a Bible, page by page and burning it. But three days later he told his scandalised father: 'A few minutes ago Jesus came into my room . . . He spoke to me. He said; "How long will you persecute me? I have come to save you. You were praying to know the right way, why do you not take it? I am the Way." He spoke to me . . . I fell at His feet.'

*Lord, is it only when you have me fall at your feet that I will hear Your voice? Only when I get rid of my prejudice, my pride . . . Lord and Holy Father, I am praying, I am falling at Your feet now.*

* * *

# 11th September

So then, just as you received Christ Jesus as Lord, continue to live in him . . . strengthened in the faith . . . and overflowing with thankfulness.

Colossians 2:6

*Gracious God, we give thanks for all you have given.*
*For Your universe – let our wonder grow.*
*For this world – teach us better stewardship of earth and sea and sky.*
*For people everywhere – let us see Your image in every human face,*
*Discern Your hand in every human culture,*

*Hear Your voice in the silence as well as the talk of neighbours.*
*For our Saviour Christ, at work in His world.*

*The Uniting Church, Australia*

*Through all eternity*
*To Thee a grateful song I'll raise:*
*But O eternity's too short*
*To utter all Thy praise!*

*Joseph Addison*

* * *

# 12th September

There is time for everything and a season for every activity under heaven.

Ecclesiastes 3:1

*Time is the steady tick of the clock,*
*Days passing by, years rolling on.*
*Time is a flower seed beginning to bloom,*
*An old man, God's plan fulfilled.*
*Time is a baby's first breath, his first smile, his first step.*
*Time is suffering and pain, trials and tribulations.*
*Time is remembering happiness, laughter, gay times.*
*Time is days past and days to come.*
*It is for a moment and for a lifetime.*
*Time is eternal.*
*Time is for rejoicing.*
*Time is for regretting.*
*Time is a gift.*
*Time is from God.*

*Anne Van Winkle*
*awaiting a kidney transplant*
*from: Me, God and the Machine*

Lord God, thank You for this day – this hour – this moment. Thank you for the life You have given me – the gift of Time within Your eternity.

* * *

# 13th September

These are the words of Him who is the First and the Last, who died and came to life again. 'I know your affliction and your poverty – yet you are rich!'

Revelation 2:9

One only has to put a toe inside hospital to see others in far worse condition. And, paradoxically, it is just when we are stripped of possessions and taken from the security of all that we are familiar with, that we come to terms with what is really important, and see how rich we are. Rich in friends, rich in hope, rich in the love and care and skill which is directed upon us, rich in the prayers of others. Money cannot buy anything that truly matters or lasts . . . Lord, how rich in blessings I am.

*When you look at others with their lands and gold,*
*Think that Christ has promised you his wealth untold:*
*Count your many blessings wealth can never buy, . . .*

*E. O. Excell*

* * *

# 14th September

To this you were called, because Christ suffered for you, leaving you an example, that you should follow His steps . . .

1 Peter 2:21

Father, I'm trying to accept with thankfulness even the discipline of uncertainty. I won't ask to see the distant scene that tomorrow will surround me . . . it's enough that You can see tomorrow. And even if You don't show me the next step I have to make, I will be content to wait . . . to stand still until I feel Your call to carry on. I can even step out into the darkness if You hold my hand. You know best. Your time and Your way for me is perfect. I praise as I follow, and I pray as I wait.

*One more step along the world I go –*
*And it's from the old I travel to the new*
*Keep me travelling along with You.*

*Sydney Carter*

* * *

# 15th September

And because the Lord had closed her womb, her rival kept provoking her. This went on year after year . . .

1 Samuel 1:6–7

Poor Hannah! A woman who dearly loved her husband, was so desperate for a child, but, year after year, remained childless. Thousands will identify with Hannah in her longing to have a baby, and will understand the longing that came close to resembling a nervous breakdown. I pray for couples who cannot have children, and also, Lord, I would pray for women who have conceived yet do not want the child they carry. Life gets to an awful pitch sometimes – I pray for some happy outcomes, like Hannah's. I pray for Your blessing on each individual to feel embraced in Your care.

*Then Hannah prayed and said:*
*My heart rejoices in the Lord;*
*There is no one holy like the Lord;*
*There is no one beside You;*
*There is no Rock like our God.*

*1 Samuel 1:1–2*

* * *

# 16th September

'I am saying nothing beyond what the prophets and Moses said would happen – that the Christ would suffer and, as the first to rise from the dead, would proclaim light to His own people and to the Gentiles.'

At this point Festus interrupted Paul's defence. 'You are out of your mind, Paul!' he shouted. 'Your great learning is driving you insane.'

'I am not insane, most excellent Festus,' Paul replied.

'What I am saying is true and reasonable . . . King Agrippa, do you believe the prophets? I know you do.'

Then Agrippa said to Paul, 'Do you think that in such a short time you can persuade me to be a Christian?'

Paul replied, 'Short time or long – I pray God that not only you but all who are listening to me today may become what I am, except for these chains.'

Acts 26:21–29

* * *

# 17th September

Jesus said: 'The king will reply, 'I tell you the truth, whatever you did for one of the least of these brothers of mine, you did for me.'

Matthew 25:40

Sometimes we take the sayings and the words of Jesus and over-spiritualise them, when we were actually meant to take them as they were written. There are so many situations that cry out for our help and input as God's people. One-parent families, sexually abused children, the aged, homosexuals, the sick and dying, widows and orphans – the list is endless. We cannot all take up every standard, and try and pioneer every cause, but let's ask the Lord what we can do to be His hands, feet and heart in our world.

Sheila Walsh

*May Your Spirit wise and holy, with His gifts our spirits bless;*
*Make us loving, joyous, peaceful, rich in goodness, gentleness,*
*Strong in self-control, and faithful, kind in thought and deed; for He teaches, 'What you do for others you are doing unto me'.*

*William C. Piggott*

* * *

# 18th September

Then the Lord said to Moses: 'Get up early in the morning, confront Pharoah and say to him, "This is what the Lord, the God of the Hebrews says . . ." '

Exodus 9:13

It takes courage as well as conviction to approach authority whether it be 'the boss', a lawyer, politician or head of state, and the majority of us never find ourselves in such a position, thankfully! Yet to our shame it is too comfortable just to plod along, minding our own business . . . not getting involved, . . . letting someone else do all the dirty work. Thank You, Lord, for those whose commitment to justice and freedom overrides their personal fear; those whose closeness to You gives them strength for each hurdle.

*Today, O God, make me brave enough to face things of which I am afraid: strong enough to overcome the temptations which try to make me do the wrong thing and not to do the right thing . . . obedient enough to obey your voice. Help me to live in purity, to speak in truth and act in love all through today.*

*Dr William Barclay*

* * *

# 19th September

Celebrate the Feast of Harvest with the first fruits of the crops you sow in your field.

Exodus 23:16

We tend to be rather insular when thinking of 'Harvest'. Today let us give thanks for the miracle of Harvests in every country, hot, cold, wet or dry – each part of the world is capable of producing a harvest. Within the church's year we are also channelled to think of Harvest only when it applies to our country, but here in Exodus we have the wise words that we should celebrate such a glorious event which began in the very fact that the people of God had enough food for another year. How little I think of harvests in China . . . in New Zealand or Israel . . . I give little heed to the daily harvest of the sea . . . Oh Lord, open my eyes, enlarge my trust in Your providence and give me joy to celebrate.

*We thank you O Lord, for all who labour to produce our food;*
*For the farmer who tills the earth and waters it*
*For those who harvest and gather the fruits of the earth*
*For those who tend the sheep and the cattle*
*For those who buy and sell*
*For all those on whose labour we daily depend for our food.*

*Wesley Ariarajah, Sri Lanka*
*(prayer written for World Food Day)*

* * *

# 20th September

Christ died for us so that, whether we are awake or asleep, we may live together with Him.

1 Thessalonians 5:10

Those superior people who can always sleep and who say loftily 'I go to bed to sleep', after our confession of a sleepless night, might sometimes ask themselves if they are paying themselves a compliment. Paul, we may comfort ourselves, confessed to many a sleepless night and knew what it was to tremble with fear and to be depressed. Yet Paul went on praying to be delivered and gave to the world his prescription: 'In nothing be anxious, but in everything by prayer and supplication with thanksgiving let your requests be made known unto God.'

Leslie Weatherhead

*When the soft dews of kindly sleep*
*My wearied eyelids gently steep,*
*Be my last thought: How sweet to rest*
*For ever on my Saviour's breast.*

*John Keble*

* * *

# 21st September

They were all trying to frighten us, thinking, 'Their hands will get too weak for the work, and it will not be completed.' But I prayed, 'Now strengthen my hands.'

Nehemiah 6:9

There can't be many people who have never woken up to wish they didn't have to go to work – it's a real bonus to enjoy work. At times every job has its tedious side, every workplace its person who somehow manages to carp and criticise, and spoil the atmosphere. Jesus and His disciples knew all about work – in the carpenter's work-shop, in the fields, in boats and the counting house. They knew all the problems of difficult customers, all the job satisfaction of work well done. Lord, in all my efforts today, strengthen my hands . . .

*Lord Jesus Christ, Help us to obey Your calling in the places where we work, in our homes and in society, that we may be quick to seize occasions of service, and wise to use them with loving care, for the honour of our Lord.*

*(New Every Morning)*

* * *

# 22nd September

God comforts us in all our troubles, so that we can comfort those in any trouble with the comforts we ourselves have received from God.

2 Corinthians 1:4

Two women were discussing their similar situations. Each had a child who had been using drugs and another child who had undergone years of sickness and near-death, and had only been saved by drastic surgery. As they chewed over the ancient question of why some people have more suffering than others, they concluded there seemed to be no clear-cut reason. But from their experiences they agreed that they had learned compassion and empathy for others, and it served to enable them in helping others who also suffered. Paul explained the value of burdens saying they are given 'to teach us not to place reliance on ourselves, but on God'.

*O Lord, we do not ask that we be spared burdens demanded by our commitment to Christ. We pray for strength to prove faithful in our discipleship of loving and caring.*

*Donna Shriver*
*Georgia USA*

* * *

# 23rd September

In the same way the Spirit helps us in our weakness. We do not know what we ought to pray, but the Spirit himself intercedes for us with groans that words cannot express. And he who searches our hearts knows the mind of the Spirit, because the Spirit intercedes for the saints in accordance with God's will. And we know that in all things God works for the good of those who love him. . . .

Who shall separate us from the love Christ? Shall trouble or hardship or persecution or famine or nakedness or danger or sword? . . .

No, in all these things we are more than conquerors through Him who loved us. For I am convinced that neither death nor life, neither angels nor demons, neither the present nor the future, nor any powers, neither height nor depth, nor anything else in all creation, will be able to separate us from the love of God that is in Christ Jesus our Lord.

Romans 8:26–28, 35–39

* * *

# 24th September

Jesus said: 'You believe in God, believe also in me. . . .'

John 14:1

I believe in God, Creator of an unfinished world, who does not decree an eternal plan of development in which we cannot take part.

I believe in Jesus Christ, who saw the world situation and who took a stand in it.

I believe in Jesus Christ, who rises for our life so that we may be liberated from the prejudices and presumptions of fear and hate, so that we may transform the world into the Kingdom of God.

I believe in the Spirit who came with Jesus into the world.

I believe in the community of all peoples . . .

I believe that it is possible to build a just peace.

I believe that a life full of meaning is possible for all;

And I believe in the future of this world of God.

A Latin American Creed (Anon)

*Dear Lord, Creator of One World, embolden the dreams of Your believers of every nationality to move together in faith, hope and love.*

* * *

# 25th September

And God raised us up with Christ . . . in order that in the coming ages He might show the incomparable riches of His grace expressed to us in Christ Jesus.

Ephesians 2:6

Just picture for a moment what a major operation would be like without anaesthetic. Today most people facing a major operation can comfort themselves by saying, 'Well, at least I shan't feel it'. You can see, I am sure, that what

I have been leading up to is this; although anaesthetic was discovered before you were born, it was discovered for you. You can benefit from it now. Sir James Simpson could not foresee your existence in the world when he discovered chloroform, but you can say with truth when about to undergo an operation: 'It was for me.' In the same way, Christ's death on the cross was for you. You can say with the hymn-writer 'For me, for me the Saviour died.'

Selwyn Hughes

*Inscribed upon the cross we see*
*In shining letters: God is Love.*
*He bears our sins upon the tree,*
*He brings us mercy from above.*

*Thomas Kelly*

* * *

# 26th September

But the fruit of the Spirit is love, joy, peace, patience, kindness, goodness, faithfulness, gentleness and self-control.

Galatians 5:22

To slowly read the list of spiritual fruits is a sobering activity. It always makes me realise how hard the Christian life is – and how differently I behave at times to the way I ought to think and behave, but I will keep trying and keep praying. Suzanna Wesley, the mother of John and Charles (not to mention the other seventeen!), once said: 'All my sufferings have concurred to promote my spiritual good. Glory be to Thee, O God.' Suffer she did with ten children dying in infancy, a husband who was imprisoned for debt, and, consequently, years of hardship. Lord, may the faith and holiness of such women renew my dedication today.

*Life brings its problems to all of us. But how can we grow – mentally or spiritually – without problems to challenge us? It is essential for the growth of a strong Christian character, displaying the fruits of the Spirit.*

*Rev George E Diggle*

* * *

# 27th September

Jesus said: 'Be perfect, therefore, as Your heavenly Father is perfect.'

Matthew 5:48

This is one of the hardest sentences Jesus spoke. How can we be perfect? Nobody is perfect – or, in the words of a rustic saying, 'All the world is queer save thee and me . . . and even thee's a little queer!' People who imagine they are right and perfect 100 per cent of the time are unbearable and due for swift awakening. So what did Jesus mean? Perhaps we should turn around our response to the command and instead of the defeatist 'I can't', make it 'I'll try'. Because we are far from perfect is no excuse to stay just as we are. If we honestly want to be changed, with God everything is possible! Lord, what a long way You have to lift me – but if we start today, tomorrow may be easier . . .

*Finish then Thy new creation,*
*Pure and spotless let us be.*
*Let us see Thy great salvation*
*Perfectly restored in Thee.*

*Charles Wesley*

* * *

# 28th September

Jesus said: 'The harvest is plentiful but the workers are few.'

Matthew 9:37

*Harvest time – thank You Lord for the Harvest time,*
*Thank You Lord for giving all we need for living,*
*Now we bring to You our grateful prayer.*

*Thank You Lord for what You give,*
*Show us now how we should live,*
*Help us to be caring, loving, giving, sharing*
*All the gifts You give us every day*

*Help us share our daily bread*
*So that the hungry may be fed:*
*Offering our labour in caring for our neighbour*
*Showing love as Jesus showed the way.*

*Martin H. J. Cooper*

The Lord said to Moses: 'Speak to the Israelites and say to them; "When you enter the land I am going to give you and you reap its harvest, bring to the priest a sheaf of the first grain you harvest . . . this is to be a lasting ordinance for the generations to come, wherever you live." '

Leviticus 23:9–12 & 14

* * *

# 29th September

Now you are the body of Christ, and each one of you is part of it. And in the church God has appointed first of all apostles . . .

1 Corinthians 12:27

What is 'church' anyway? It isn't really a building or an organisation. It is the Christian family meeting together. Paul wrote his letters in the New Testament to congregations or groups of Christians in different places: so the church is just a number of Christians in one place, coming together like a family, to worship God. Church is 'home', too, for the Christian. For me, that means family loyalty is involved. It won't do to go from church to church trying to find one that 'suits' you, or just for a change. Loyalty to the family means being committed to one group of Christians in one place.

Cliff Richard

*The church's one foundation*
*Is Jesus Christ, her Lord.*

*Samuel J. Stone*

* * *

# 30th September

Now the body is not made up of one part but many. . . . The eye cannot say to the hand, 'I don't need you!', and the head cannot say to the feet, 'I don't need you!' On the contrary, those parts of the body that seem to be weaker are indispensable and the parts that we think are less honourable we treat with special honour. And the parts that are unpresentable are treated with special modesty, while our presentable parts need no special treatment. But God has combined the members of the body and has given greater honour to the parts that lacked it, so that there should be no division in the body, but that its parts should have equal concern for each other. If one part suffers, every part suffers with it; if one part is honoured, every part rejoices with it.

Now you are the body of Christ, and each one of you is part of it.

1 Corinthians 12:14, 21–17

* * *

# 1st October

Above all love each other deeply, because love covers a multitude of sins.

1 Peter 4:8

Love is called the fruit of the Holy Spirit, because it is to us a very product of the Tree of Life – the spirit of God Himself, grafted upon our spirits, and dwelling in us by His great mercy. Poverty enriches it, humiliation exalts it, tears gladden it, deprivation strengthens it, renunciation becomes sweet to it, and all manner of trial is welcome, inasmuch as its best life is to die for Christ. Thus love is at once a virtue, a gift, a fruit and a beatitude.

St Francois de Sales

*And the God of all grace, who called you to His eternal glory in Christ, after you have suffered a little while, will Himself restore you and make you strong, firm and steadfast. To Him be the power for ever and ever, Amen.*

*1 Peter 5:10–11*

* * *

# 2nd October

Train a child in the way he should go, and when he is old he will not turn from it.

Proverbs 22:6

In infancy, before I could speak, I heard a particular language. As water was sprinkled on my head, I was received into the family of Christ. The precious sign of the cross was traced on my brow. Before I could speak, I was asked to walk with God all the days of my life. As others answered for me, I heard the language of love, without understanding I heard my parents pray. And as I learned to speak, so I learned prayers, prayers that would never leave me.

Frank Topping

*Lord I pray for those who have taken their children to be blessed and received into the great family of worshipping people. May those homes be homes of security, love, learning and growing in grace.*

* * *

# 3rd October

The virgin will be with child and will give birth to a son, and they will call him Emmanuel – which means, God with us.

Matthew 1:23

Forty years ago when I was struggling with the decision to enter the ministry, I was walking through the woods near Mountain Lake Park, Maryland. Near the path I spotted a memory verse card, dropped perhaps by a child going home from Sunday school. Through all these years its message has been the strength of my life: 'Lo I am with you alway, even unto the end of the world.' After many years as chaplain to the military, through war and peace, I know that nothing else matters – programmes, reports, promotions and all the rest – without that assurance of His presence. How wonderful! God is with us!

Rev Meredith P. Smith
Washington DC

*Lord, on my knees, I beg to know the assurance . . . I cling on to Your promise and it gives me strength for the next hour.*

* * *

# 4th October

Let the word of Christ dwell in you richly as you teach and admonish one another . . . as you sing psalms, hymns and spiritual songs with gratitude in your hearts to God.

Colossians 3:16

On 4 October 1738 two young clergymen brothers went to visit the internationally acclaimed Dr Isaac Watts. Elderly Dr Watts was nearing the close of the hymn-writing which had made him so famous and the Wesley brothers were just at the beginning of what would be their life's work. Thank You Lord, that Your work and the witness of believers carries on from generation to generation – thank You for the poetic gifts of Isaac Watts and Charles Wesley and the writers of today, who find fresh inspiration to express Your eternal love and power. Give me joy as I sing . . .

*I sing the almighty power of God*
*That made the mountains rise,*
*That spread the flowing seas abroad*
*And built the lofty skies.*

*Isaac Watts*

* * *

# 5th October

Give thanks to the Lord. Sing to Him a new song, play skilfully and shout in triumph:

Psalm 33:3

*Come to us, creative Spirit,*
*In our Father's house,*
*Every natural talent foster*
*Hidden skills arouse,*
*That within Your earthly temple*
*Wise and simple may rejoice.*

*Poet, painter, music-maker,*
*All your treasures bring;*
*Craftsman, actor, graceful dancer,*
*Make your offering.*
*Join your hands in celebration!*
*Let creation shout and sing!*

*In all places and for ever*
*Glory be expressed*
*To the Son, with God the Father*
*And the Spirit blest.*
*In our worship and our living*
*Keep us striving towards the best.*

*David Mowbray*

Lord, thank You for the joy of music, of paintings, of dancing . . . all the ways that artistic vision enriches life and worship.

* * *

# 6th October

Let the peace of Christ rule in your hearts and be thankful.

Colossians 3:15

Teenager Henry Alford was 16 when he gave his life to

the service of Jesus Christ. In his own words, he wrote: 'Henceforth to become His and to do His work as far as in me lies.' Born on 7 October 1810, Henry was a multi-talented young man. Apart from becoming ordained he wrote poetry, hymns, translations of the Bible and lectured, not to mention his fine painting and musical knowledge. Whilst Dean of Caterbury Cathedral, he wrote a hymn of praise and gladness which brings Christians to their feet at harvest festivals the world over.

*Come, ye thankful people come,*
*Raise the song of harvest home!*
*All is safely gathered in*
*Ere the winter storms begin.*
*God our maker doth provide*
*For our wants to be supplied:*
*Come to God's own temple, come*
*Raise the song of harvest-home!*

*Henry Alford*

* * *

# 7th October

Carry each other's burdens, and in this way you will fulfil the law of Christ. If anyone thinks he is something when he is nothing, he deceives himself. Each one should test his own actions. Then he can take pride in himself without comparing himself to somebody else, for each one should carry his own load . . . Do not be deceived: God cannot be mocked. A man reaps what he sows. The one who sows to please his sinful nature, from that nature will reap destruction; the one who sows to please the spirit, from the spirit will reap eternal life. Let us not become weary in doing good, for at the proper time we will reap a harvest if we do not give up. Therefore, as we have opportunity, let us do good to all people, especially to those who belong to the family of believers.

Galations 6:2–10

* * *

# 8th October

The earth is the Lord's and everything in it, the world and all who live in it.

Psalm 24:1

*We mine the copper, gold and iron*
*We take the minerals from the earth*
*Coal, wood and water; soil and clay.*
*We use these gifts from day to day*
*But*
*Not ours O Lord, they're Yours:*
*The earth belongs to You.*
*From orchard tree and soft brown earth*
*From bush and cane, from branch and stalk*
*From rivers, seas and grinding mill*
*We take all good things as we will*
*But*
*Not ours O lord, they're Yours*
*The earth belongs to You.*

(*from a Word in Season*, compiled by Donald Hilton N.C.E.C.)

Thank you Lord that I live in such a fantastic world that I can never see, understand or appreciate all that lives, grows and multiplies. Help me today to look with new eyes on all the good things that surround me, food, warmth, clothing, fabrics, water. Give me a new heart to soak in Your love

* * *

# 9th October

Now when Jesus saw the crowds, He went up on a mountainside and sat down. His disciples came to Him and He began to teach them:

Matthew 5:1

We are for ever talking about the good life! 'Have a good time!' we say. Much of what Jesus said to His little group of young men – His 'cell' of revolutionaries, who were to transvaluate all values, was on the good life. The heart of it is concentrated in the hilltop talk which we call 'The Sermon on the Mount'. Many folk, with thoughtless phonographic repetition of cliches, speak of that Sermon as impossible idealism. Most of it, however, on the contrary, simply exposes the granite rock of ultimate reality, rooted in the foundation of the universe. Life would be changed if we gained power from Him to forsake our materialistic 'success' delusions and live by these shining, central facts.

Basil Mathews

*Stay Master, stay upon that heavenly hill:*
*A little longer let us linger still:*
*At God's own feet our spirits seek their rest;*
*And he is nearest Him who serves Him best.*

*Samuel Greg*

* * *

# 10th October

When Esau was forty years old, he married Judith daughter of Beeri the Hittite, and also Basemath, daughter of Elon the Hittite. They were a source of grief to Isaac and Rebekah.

Genesis 26:34

The briefest of phrases but therein lies the reason for Rebekah's deception of her husband in robbing Esau of his birthright. She didn't get on with her daughters-in-law! In fact, both Isaac and Rebekah had taken a dim view of the marriages to Hittite women. So Rebekah was an unhappy woman: disappointed by her elder son and showing obvious favouritism to her youngest, Jacob, and out of these throbbing emotions comes the story of trickery and tragedy. Favouritism is still a major cause of distress and how many mothers are unhappy with their son's choice of bride? Lord, I am a woman: a turbulent mixture of motives and feelings – help me through the tangle of relationships and keep me loving and honest.

*As man and woman we were made,*
*That love be found and life begun:*
*Praise for the love that comes to life*
*Through child or parent, man or wife.*

*Brian Wren*

* * *

# 11th October

They celebrated the feast of Tabernacles with the required number of burnt offerings . . . as well as those brought as freewill offerings for the Lord.

Ezra 3:4–5

*Dear Lord,*
*I offer myself to You:*
*My mind – to think for You:*
*My eyes – to see the needs of others;*
*My ears – to hear the world's cries;*
*My voice – to speak for You;*
*My hands – to work for Your kingdom;*
*My feet – to walk in Your path;*
*My life – to be used in Your service;*
*My heart – to love you above all. Amen*

*Network Prayer*

O God, what offering shall I give to Thee, the Lord of earth and skies? My spirit, soul and flesh receive.

A holy, living sacrifice. Small as it is – 'tis all my store; More should'st Thou have if I had more.

Joachim Lange

* * *

# 12th October

Jesus said: 'But you will receive power when the Holy Spirit comes on you;'

Acts 1:8

The Capitol Hill luncheon in honour of Mother Teresa was held in the ornately decorated Senate caucus room in the Russell Building . . . Here was a woman who obviously had tremendous power . . . She had more power than I had seen in this city of power. How had she done this? She owned nothing, never shook her fist in anger for her rights, and never asked for anything for herself. Instead she had reached down into the gutter and raised up and loved those the world calls unlovable. And she had done this simply because the poor were created by the God she loves and serves.

Dee Jepsen

*The power to win a soul for God*
*The Spirit too imparts;*
*And he the gift of Christ our Lord,*
*Dwells now in all our hearts.*

*El Nathan*

* * *

# 13th October

Be devoted to one another in brotherly love. Honour one another above yourselves.

Romans 12:10

*Let there be love shared among us*
*Let there be love in our eyes,*
*May now Your love sweep this nation*
*Cause us O Lord to arise –*
*Give us a fresh understanding*
*Of brotherly love that is real:*
*Let there be love shared among us*
*Let there be love.*

*D. Bilbrough*

Dear Lord, as I approach the meditations for and the challenges of One World Week I earnestly pray for understanding and love to grow in families, between colours and creeds, young and old throughout Your world.

* * *

# 14th October

And now brothers, we want you to know about the grace that God has given the Macedonian churches. Out of the most severe trial, their overflowing joy and their extreme poverty welled up in rich generosity. For I testify that they gave as much as they were able, and even beyond their ability. Entirely on their own, they urgently pleaded with us for the privilege of sharing in this service to the saints. And, they did not do as we expected, but they gave themselves first to the Lord and then to us in keeping with God's will. . . . Just as you excel in everything – in faith, in speech, in knowledge, in complete earnestness and in your love for us – see that you also excel in this grace of giving.

For you know the grace of our Lord Jesus Christ, that though he was rich, yet for your sakes He became poor, so that you through His poverty you might become rich.

Paul writing to the Corinthian church
2 Corinthians 8:1–5, 7 & 9

* * *

# 15th October

Or take ships as an example. Although they are so large and are driven by strong winds, they are steered by a very small rudder.

James 3:4

I'm thinking of three kinds of ships today – friendSHIP, worSHIP and stewardSHIP. Like the great ships on the oceans, so these 'ships' of our emotional and spiritual action sail on the ocean of our life – they can be blown off course by tiny words of mistrust or envy or anger . . . they can be shipwrecked on rocks of divorce, unemployment, stresses and burdens. Lord, I bring You my friendships, I give You my worship, and I pray for Your wisdom to guide me in stewardship of the people and things within my care. O still, small voice be the rudder which steers my life.

*Thank You Father for the friendships which warm my heart –*
*Thank You Jesus, Holy Son for worship which lifts my soul*
*Thank You, Holy Spirit for the fulfilment and challenge of stewardship.*

* * *

# 16th October

The body is a unit, though it is made up of many parts; and though all its parts are many, they form one body. So it is with Christ.

1 Corinthians 12:12

I never cease to be amazed at the difference between people. Yet we are pretty limited in make-up: just a pair of legs, arms, body, head with sundry features of eyes, nose, etc., etc. The millions of permutations are staggering. Apart from the physical differences, we have the intellectual and spiritual inclinations that divide as much as race and culture. Lord, You died for all irrespective of who, where and why . . . open my heart to the Gospel teaching that despite our many varieties we are all one in Christ Jesus, Lord of all.

*We need each other. Although some of us may be experiencing wonderful times when everything in life is great, other brothers and sisters may not be doing as well. They need our help and support. That's what the body of Christ is for.*

*Luis Palau*

* * *

# 17th October

Here is a trustworthy saying that deserves full acceptance: 'Christ Jesus came into the world to save sinners' . . .

1 Timothy 1:15

*I cannot tell why Jesus came to save me,*
*When I do all the things that hurt Him so;*
*Or why He pours His tender love around me*
*To guide me in the way I ought to go.*
*But this I know – He changed my life completely –*
*He warmed my heart with tongues of fire divine,*
*And now I know His presence always with me*
*For this, the Saviour, Saviour of the World, is mine!*

*E.R.*

Christ Jesus came into the world to save sinners: hear then the word of Grace: Your sins are forgiven!

From the Communion Service

* * *

# 18th October

Jesus said to them: 'Why are you troubled and why do doubts rise in your minds?'

Luke 24:38

The German philosopher Nietzsche said: 'Show me that you are redeemed and then I will believe in your redeemer.' And, indeed, it makes us stop and think – our Christian example is too often fuzzy and confused to those who are cold to the claims of the gospel. Martin Luther once arrived home to find his wife dressed in the black of mourning and he was concerned to know who had died. His wife said simply she was mourning for God because Martin looked as though his God was dead. Lord, I ask for a new vision of the power of the Gospel, a clearer insight into the power of joy, the unshakeable calm of trust . . . I claim Your promises, Lord, and pray You will make me a conqueror over my troubles and doubts for Your name's sake.

*. . . the majority of Christians are just as worried as anyone else . . . not noticeably more able to cope with life than anyone else. Christianity will only become effective when Christians become as Christian as their claims.*

*Dr William Barclay*

* * *

# 19th October

Jesus said: 'Go! I am sending you out like lambs among wolves.'

Luke 10:3

On 19 October 1836, an 11-year-old Maori girl was brutally murdered in a tribal ambush. As a grim trophy of their kill, the Arawa warriors took the little girl's gospel back to their home in Rotorua. But back home no one could read.

After some time a slave was captured and brought to the house of the man who had killed Tarore – the slave could read and he read to his new master the words of Jesus as found in Luke's gospel. The man suddenly knew that God was speaking to him – he felt devastated at the murder he had committed and sent a message to Tarore's father, begging for forgiveness. Tarore's father, Chief Ngakuku, forgave his enemy and peace came to the two tribes. The slave kept Tarore's gospel, and God used him to bring many to find Jesus as their Saviour. Years later, European Christians were surprised at how many Maoris could quote from Luke's gospel!

*Jesus, tender shepherd, hear me –*
*Bless Thy little lamb tonight . . .*

*Mary Duncan*

* * *

# 20th October

When a man's ways are pleasing to the Lord, he makes even his enemies live at peace with him.

Proverbs 16:7

It takes two to quarrel. If one of the two exudes goodwill, comes with good cheer, gives of himself in selfless love, that one is at peace. The other may still despise, hate, and abuse the first, but he remains the one with the problem, the one with the inner darkness and despair. As God's people of peace we need not be victimised by our detractors. We can be at peace with them as Christ was, even if they are at odds with us. God calls us to be 'big' people, strong people, serene people, steady, solid people – we are not to be dragged down into the ditch of destructive hatreds, animosities and mudslinging.

W. Phillip Keller

*Take from our souls the strain and stress*
*And let our ordered lives confess*
*The beauty of Thy peace.*

*John G. Whittier*

* * *

# 21st October

Therefore each of you must put off falsehood and speak truthfully to his neighbour, for we are all members of one body. In your anger do not sin. Do not let the sun go down while you are angry, and do not give the devil a foothold . . . Do not let any unwholesome talk come out of your mouths, but only what is helpful for building others up according to their needs, that it may benefit those who listen . . . Get rid of all bitterness, rage and anger, brawling and slander, along with every form of malice. Be kind and compassionate to one another, forgiving each other, just as in Christ God forgave you.

Be imitators of God, therefore, as dearly loved children and live a life of love, just as Jesus Christ loved us and gave himself up for us as a fragrant offering and sacrifice to God.

Ephesians 4:25–32 & 5:1

* * *

# 22nd October

Thinking He was the gardener, she said: 'Sir, if you carried Him away, tell me where you have put Him . . .

John 20:15

There is hardly a day in my life when I do not consult my Bible. But the passages I am drawn to vary as my circumstances change – that is the Bible's strength: it is a book for all seasons.

Lately I have come back again and again to John 20, 15. Mary Magdalene, who knew Jesus intimately, did not at first recognise the risen Christ. To her, He could have been the gardener. And as we read on, by the lakeside and on the road to Emmaus, we find the same mystery . . . He was no longer the particular Jesus, He was Everyman. His death had made Him more like the rest of us. This tells me we may still meet Him anywhere, in anyone – a man by a lake, a stranger on the road, a gardener.

Gerald Priestland

*When Mary in the garden walked*
*And with her risen master talked:*
*And friend to friend in wonder said*
*The Lord is risen from the dead.*

*W. H. Hamilton*

* * *

# 23rd October

It is for freedom that Christ has set us free. Stand firm then –

Galatians 5:1

Racial harmony is often determined on our willingness to accept each other. This does not mean uniformity, nor compromise of our beliefs, but it does call for our positive steps to understand that we are all made in the image of

God, that Christ's blood was sacrificed for all, and that His blood has set us free from the prejudices and mistrust which would divide. With the establishment of a One World Week I strive not to feel patronising towards the underdeveloped countries. Lord, I have so much to learn from their generosity, their openness, their genuine joy and hope in freedom for their lands and worship.

*God, our Father and our Mother, creator and sustainer of the universe, we thank You for the wondrous ways in which You have revealed Your love . . . we pray that You will pour Your love into our hearts that with open minds we may accept all peoples of the world as brothers and sisters so that all mankind may find the joy of true freedom in You.*

*Rev Dr Swaminathan Jacob (Asia)*

* * *

# 24th October

By faith Abraham made his home in the promised land like a stranger in a foreign country:

Hebrews 1:9

*Lord, I am a stranger, yet still I am at home;*
*at home with my brothers and sisters in Christ;*
*at home when I meet with them in worship . . .*
*at home as I share with them the bread that is Your body,*
*the wine that is Your blood,*
*dissolving all differences of race and tongue,*
*class and custom, wealth and education,*
*reconciling all wrongs done by one nation to another*
*liberating us from all our past.*
*For in You we are all one*
*and nothing can separate us from the love of Christ.*

*David G. Temple*

*The love that made us makes us one*
*And strangers now are friends.*

*Brian A. Wren*

* * *

## 25th October

Get ready; be prepared . . .

Ezekiel 38:7

Be prepared! Not just a whimsical phrase left over from the Boy Scouts . . . not just the exhortation of the prophet Ezekiel. Our days would run a whole lot smoother if we actually did prepare ourselves. Prepare ourselves to be misunderstood, to be passed over, to be hurt, to feel alone, to admit our fault. Lord help me to be prepared to swallow my pride, to start again. I need to be ready and open to listen to Your promptings within my heart.

Remind the people . . . to be obedient, to be ready to do whatever is good, to slander no one, to be peaceable and considerate, and to show true humility towards all men.

Titus 3:1–2

* * *

## 26th October

While your servant was busy here and there, the man disappeared!

1 Kings 20:40

Rather a dismal excuse . . . a servant given charge of a prisoner and the prisoner escaped while the servant was 'busy here and there'. Yet there is a parallel here for your lives – we are given charge of days and people yet we can be so busy here and there that the days evaporate before we realise, and suddenly when we glance at the children they are adults, the parents are aged, the partner has grown away. Lord, I don't mean to be preoccupied – I pray for the gift of making time for those I love, having time to make the most of each day. Busyness won't be my excuse today.

*But Martha was distracted by all the preparations that had to be made. She came to Jesus and asked, 'Lord, don't you care that my sister has left me to do the work by myself? Tell her to help me.' 'Martha, Martha,' the Lord said . . . Mary has chosen what is better!'*

*Luke 10:40–42*

* * *

# 27th October

Another of His disciples, Andrew, Simon Peter's brother, spoke up, 'Here is a boy with five small barley loaves and two small fish . . .'

John 6:8

In just the brief sentences about Andrew, in the gospels, he comes across as a friendly and outgoing character. It was Andrew who took his brother Simon Peter to meet Jesus, and, in the quotation above, we see it was Andrew that took the boy with the loaves and fish to Jesus. Andrew was a good 'introducer'. And how much we depend on people like that to be good mixers, to break the ice, to make sure people do not feel alone in situations. Lord, I ask for the thoughtfulness and friendliness of Andrew. Above all, when an opportunity arises, help me to introduce someone to Jesus, my friend, and that He will use us to spread His love and care throughout the community.

*Lord, I bring by name my friends in prayer*
*I lift to You the hearts and minds in need:*
*With all an Andrew's introduction share –*
*For friend and stranger intercede.*

* * *

# 28th October

For we do not preach ourselves, but Jesus Christ as Lord, and ourselves as your servants for Jesus' sake. For God, who said, 'Let Light shine out of darkness,' made His Light shine in our hearts to give us the light of the knowledge of the glory of God in the face of Christ.

But we have this treasure in jars of clay to show that this all surpassing power is from God and not from us. We are hard pressed on every side, but not crushed; perplexed, but not in despair; persecuted, but not abandoned; struck down but not destroyed.

We always carry around in our body the death of Jesus so that the life of Jesus may also be revealed in our body. So then, death is at work in us, but life is at work in you . . . therefore we do not lose heart.

2 Corinthians 4:5–11 & 18

* * *

# 29th October

Jesus said: 'I am the living bread that came down from heaven. If a man eats of this bread he will live for ever.'

John 6:51

A husband whose wife was in hospital having their second baby was left in charge of the home and the shopping. When she returned from hospital most things had been taken care of, but she also found a peculiar assortment of left-overs in the bread bin, ranging from hard crust to green mould. This living parable came home to that Canadian couple as the husband realised:

'I would say we have sometimes presented to hungry souls a Christ cut into the neat slices of our creeds, packaged in the wrappings of our formal services, dried up with our dignity, unacceptably stale by our stuffiness and inactivity. We have said: Take, eat – this is Christ! And it isn't. For Christ is alive – fresh – life giving and nourishing.'

*We taste Thee O Thou living bread*
*And long to feast upon Thee still . . .*
*Bernard of Clairvaux, 1091–1153*

* * *

# 30th October

I will sing of your love and justice; to You, O Lord, I will sing praise.

Psalm 101:1

A few nights after the death of my husband I woke and peered automatically at the digital clock. The time glowed 5.13. Yet instead of registering the time in my mind, I immediately thought of hymn number 513 in the old Methodist Hymn Book I had grown up with. Well-known words flooded into me which suddenly held new meaning and gave me a certain peace and new confidence that the eternal arms of Love were around me to hold and keep me through the darkest valley of my life. I was able to thank God for the inspiration of hymn writers whose words give expression to our inexpressible longings.

*I long for household voices gone*
*For vanished smiles I long;*
*But God has led my dear ones on*
*And He can do no wrong.*

*I know not what the future has*
*Of marvel or surprise:*
*Assured alone that life and death*
*His mercy underlies.*

*John Greenleaf Whittier*
*(513 in Methodist Hymn Book)*

* * *

# 31st October

For our struggle is not against flesh and blood, but against the rulers, against the authorities, against the powers of this dark world and against the spiritual forces of evil . . .

Ephesians 6:12

A widespread and intense interest in occult powers and

practices confronts us everywhere. Popular magazines feature articles about black and white magic and profile the lives of well-known seers. . . . Newspapers provide daily astrology readings and broad coverage of cults that worship Satan. . . . Today we see the foolish hearts of man darkened by the ceaseless activity of this host of seducing spirits. . . . For us to know our enemy and his tactics is the beginning of our sharing in God's victory over him (Satan) through the Lord Jesus Christ!

David Watson

*Lord, I'm fuzzy in my condemnation of 'evil' – I don't want to make a fuss . . . forgive me that I commit the sin of underestimating the powers of evil and the insidious grip these forces have on each life. Heal me, strengthen me, guide me, protect me.*

* * *

# 1st November

We are hard pressed on every side, but not crushed; perplexed but not in despair . . .

2 Corinthians 4:8

Many Christians today talk about the 'difficulties of our times' as though we should have to wait for better ones before the Christian religion can take root. It is heartening to remember that this faith took root and flourished amazingly in conditions that would have killed anything less vital in a matter of weeks. These early Christians were on fire with the conviction that they had become, through Christ, literally sons of God; they were pioneers of a new humanity, founders of a new Kingdom. They still speak to us across the centuries. Perhaps if we believed what they believed, we might achieve what they achieved.

J. B. Phillips

*Have we trials and temptations?*
*Is there trouble anywhere?*
*We should never be discouraged:*
*Take it to the Lord in prayer.*

*Joseph M. Scriven*

* * *

# 2nd November

Jesus said: 'What shall we say the kingdom of God is like?'

Mark 4:30

*The sky is grey and chilly, and the plain is frozen hard.*
*The warmth of sunlight is gone*
*From the barren and dark street of the poor.*
*From where did they come, those drawn and haggard faces?*
*For what are they searching, those eyes, those emaciated hands?*
*Oh Lord, now come to us*
*Be with us together in this place.*

*Ah – this street, this lonely street*
*Where outstretched hands are rejected,*
*Oh where can it be, the Kingdom of Heaven?*
*Can we find it in the thick clouds that hover over the place of death?*
*Oh Lord, now come to us here*
*Be with us together in this place.*

*Songs of the Minjung*
*Ecumenical Youth Council in Korea.*

Jesus looked at him (the ruler) and said: 'How hard it is for the rich to enter the Kingdom of God.'

Luke 18:24

* * *

# 3rd November

I have been crucified with Christ, and I no longer live, but Christ lives in me.

Galations 2:20

North Korean soldiers captured a Salvation Army officer. They marched him into the village square and ordered him to denounce both his faith and his uniform. Holding the Bible high for all to see, the Salvationist cried: 'It doesn't matter whether I live or die – but Christ lives!' He refused all threats of torture and was shot dead where he stood, his Bible held fast in his hand.

*Christ is alive! Let Christians sing*
*His cross stands empty to the sky,*
*Let streets and homes with praises ring*
*His love in death shall never die.*

*Brian Wren*

* * *

# 4th November

If you have any encouragement from being united with Christ, if any comfort from His love, if any fellowship with the Spirit, if any tenderness and compassion, then make my joy complete by being like-minded, having the same love, being one in spirit and purpose. Do nothing out of selfish ambition or vain conceit, but in humility consider others better than yourselves. Each of you should not look to your own interests, but also to the interests of others. Your attitude should be the same as that of Jesus Christ:
Who, being in very nature God,
did not consider equality with God
something to be grasped,
but made Himself nothing,
taking the very nature of a servant,
being made in human likeness.

Philippians 2:1–7

* * *

# 5th November

Love is patient, love is kind.

1 Corinthians 13:4

Thank You, Lord, for so many acts of kindness . . . the man who gave me a lift when I had missed the bus; the phone call to wish me well before an important interview;

the letter of sympathy when I had lost a dear one. A friend dropped in and listened when I needed someone to talk to; the neighbour who brought a home-baked pie when we had sickness in the house . . . Lord, part of your plan for me is that I should be on the alert to offer deeds of kindness, that day by day as I receive Your love, I may learn new ways to give it away.

Rev Peter Bolt

*Lord and Saviour, true and kind*
*Be the master of my mind. . . .*
*Till my whole glad nature be*
*Trained for duty and for Thee.*

*H. C. G. Moule*

* * *

# 6th November

I never sat in the company of revellers, never made merry with them; I sat alone . . .

Jeremiah 15:17

In the gregarious, 'instant' society of these last years of the 20th century, the problem of loneliness has never been greater. The prophet Jeremiah knew what it was like to sit alone – my prayers today are for those who sit alone and long for a cheerful voice or a friendly smile: my prayers are also for those who make 'talking-tapes' for the blind and the housebound; who read newspapers onto tape for them and bring into their lives some humour or revive memories.

*In the streets of every city*
*Where the bruised and lonely dwell,*
*Let us show the Saviour's pity*
*Let us of His mercy tell.*

*Hugh Sherlock*

* * *

# 7th November

Jesus said: 'For if you forgive men when they sin against you, your heavenly Father will also forgive you. . . .'
Matthew 6:15

*On the table side by side,*
*The Holy Bible and the T.V. guide,*
*One is well-worn but cherished with pride.*
*(Not the Bible – but the T.V. guide).*
*One is used daily to help folk decide,*
*No! it isn't the Bible, it's the T.V. guide.*
*As pages are turned, what shall we see,*
*Oh, what does it matter, turn on the T.V.*
*So they open the book in which they confide.*
*(No, not the Bible, it's the T.V. guide).*
*The word of God is seldom read,*
*Maybe a verse as they fall into bed,*
*Exhausted and sleepy and tired as can be,*
*Not from reading the Bible, from watching T.V.*
*So then back on the table, side by side,*
*Is the Holy Bible and the T.V. guide,*
*No time for prayer, not time for the word,*
*The Plan of salvation is seldom heard,*
*Forgiveness for sin so full and free,*
*Is found in the Bible, not on T.V.!*

*Anon*

Lord, I know that without Your guidance I am going to be floundering unless I learn Your ways, my dealings with people will be lacking. Guide me, guard me, love me and forgive me.

* * *

# 8th November

When the child (Moses) grew older, she took him to Pharoah's daughter and he became her son.
Exodus 2:10

In her adoption of Moses, Pharoah's daughter gave him

the very best start for life – money, education, authority and very probably a great deal of affection as well. Her heart must have been heavy when her 'son' spurned the Egyptian way of life and worship, and returned to his own people, ultimately to lead them out of captivity. In any situation adoption has many problems for both parties involved. Lord, my prayer today is for all couples who have, or are about to adopt – and for the babies or children they take to their hearts. May understanding bridge the divide of race and colour and disadvantage . . . may love be the overwhelming force to seal the relationship: motivated and rooted in Your love.

*Gracious Father, Gracious Father*
*We're so glad to be Your children:*

*Jimmy Owens*

* * *

# 9th November

Then the disciples prayed: 'Lord, You know everyone's heart.'

Acts 1:24

This short prayer in Acts is very revealing in that it's not a prayer of panic, but one of absolute trust. The disciples came before, God accepting that He knew best and therefore the outcome of their momentary dilemma was bound to be His will. I am often guilty of tumbling out of my prayers in a fashion that tells God what I think would be best first . . . forgive me, Lord, give me the faith to open myself to Your direction, knowing that You know my heart better than I do myself . . . take my heart, not my arguments and persuasion . . . I give my heart freely and for always.

*The heart has its reasons, which reason knows not, as we feel in a thousand instances. It is the heart which is conscious of God, not the reason. This then is faith: God sensible to the heart, not to the reason.*

*Blaise Pascal*

* * *

# 10th November

The man who had received five talents went at once and put his money to work and gained five more.

Matthew 25:16

The American heart surgeon Lyle Damon-Joyce was asked if he thought a person's faith had anything to do with their recovery. He answered: 'Definitely. I think that people who are at ease and at rest with God enter an operation with much less anxiety. And many times that lack of anxiety is crucial. We don't understand the chemistry of anxiety but there is no question that it is real. God gave me a job to do – He has given me a skill and He expects me to use it. To understand what God wants I have to walk as closely to Him as I can. I have a gift – but it's no different from the gift God gives to the carpenter or the mechanic: He expects us to do our best with what He has given us.'

*The Master replied: 'Well done, good and faithful servant. You have been faithful with a few things, I will put you in charge of many things.'*

*Matthew 25: 21*

* * *

# 11th November

Keep on loving each other as brothers. Do not forget to entertain strangers, for by so doing some people have entertained angels without knowing it. Remember those in prison as if you were their fellow prisoners, and those who are ill-treated as if you yourselves were suffering.

Marriage should be honoured by all, and the marriage bed kept pure, for God will judge the adulterer and all the sexually immoral. Keep your lives free from the love of money and be content with what you have, because God has said:

'Never will I leave you;
never will I forsake you'.
So we say with confidence:
'The Lord is my helper
I will not be afraid.'

Hebrews 13:1–6

* * *

# 12th November

For the message of the cross is foolishness to those who are perishing, but to us who are being saved it is the power of God.

1 Corinthians 1:18

We had known the great God of the churches and of the cathedrals – the God of splendid worship – the God in majesty and glory – and we had been right. This God is truly our God. But when the Russian emigres found themselves deprived of all glory, void of all greatness . . . they discovered God as they had always known Him by faith in the Gospel but seldom experienced within their lives. . . . Defeated as we were, this God . . . had taken up defeat to make defeat itself a way of achievement.

Anthony Bloom

*Christ is risen!*
*Henceforth never death nor hell shall us enthrall,*
*We are Christ's,*
*In Him for ever we have triumphed over all.*

*J. S. B. Monsell*

* * *

# 13th November

But the Lord stood at my side and gave me strength.

2 Timothy 4:17

It wasn't that the Christian men and women in the internment camp were outstanding in their goodness and their personalities, but having worshipped God together in fellowship behind wires, they knew one another in that which was eternal. They received the energy of each other's friendship to help them live their daily lives, to keep before their eyes the eternal values which the camp conditions had brought into new relief. There were among us the few, mostly humble folk, who were being constantly drawn upon by others; yet their spiritual reservoirs were deep, so that the more they gave the more they seemed to have, for they themselves knew the secret of drawing upon God.

William Sewell

*O strengthen me, that while I stand*
*Firm on the rock, and strong in Thee,*
*I may stretch out a loving hand*
*To wrestlers with the troubled sea.*

*Frances Ridley Havergal*

* * *

# 14th November

Jesus said: 'Father forgive them, for they do not know what they are doing.'

Luke 23:34

Who hasn't experienced deep hurt – the seething resentment that blocks out the balm of forgiveness? One of the great divides between Christ Jesus and His followers in every generation is the human stubborness and refusal to forgive. 'Father forgive . . . These words are inscribed in Coventry Cathedral which was bombed so viciously on 14 November 1940. Today the 'new' cathedral stands risen from the ruins to new life and a witness cleansed of bitterness. 'Father forgive . . .' O Lord God, into the emotional void of my churning mind breathe the forgiveness of Your Spirit . . . forgive me, then help me to forgive too.

*Dear Lord and Father of mankind*
*Forgive our foolish ways.*

*J. G. Whittier*

* * *

# 15th November

'But what about you,' Jesus asked. 'Who do you say I am?'

Mark 8:29

Commissioner Catherine Bramwell-Booth was asked about moments of doubt or questioning: with characteristic bluntness she replied: 'Oh, I had questioning all my life in a way. I do now. The devil knows how to attack me. By nature I'm an unbeliever. Every now and then it sweeps over me; How can this be? How can that be? But the Lord Jesus becomes real and once He becomes real to you – you must excuse the way I put it – you can't get rid of Him. Every time – there's Christ. I feel I put great importance on the question the Lord put to the disciples; 'Whom say ye that I am?' I feel that every person who hears about Christ, sooner or later, comes up to that question. Who is He?

*You are the King of Glory*
*You are the Prince of Peace*
*You are the Lord of Heaven and Earth*
*You're the Son of Righteousness*
*You have the words of Eternal Life*
*You are Jesus Christ the Lord!*

*M. Ford*

* * *

# 16th November

Here I am. I stand at the door and knock. If anyone hears my voice and opens the door, I will go in. . . .

Revelation 3:20

The famous painting of Christ the Light of the World, by Holman Hunt, depicts Christ standing outside a handleless door. The explanation for this has been given that God never foists Himself upon us – He waits to be asked to enter our lives. The free will is ours and we can either accept or reject His everlasting love. Lord, at times I'm not listening for Your knock and sometimes I even pretend I haven't heard Your knock. I want all Your goodness and life flooding into my heart but I'm afraid of commitment, afraid of letting go of myself. . . .

*I bring you joy from heaven above:*
*I bring you pardon peace and love –*
*Say, weary heart, oppressed with sin,*
*May I come in, may I come in?*
*Frances Jane van Alstyne*

* * *

# 17th November

Therefore, prepare your minds for action; be self-controlled; set your hope fully on the grace to be given you when Jesus Christ is revealed.
1 Peter 1:13

However progressive and enlightened the educational system, schools still have the basic duties of teaching the three R's – the time-honoured Reading, wRiting and 'Rithmetic. And nobody gets very far without the basics. Spiritual education is not less concerned with basics and there are three R's for the Christian pupil too. Jesus Christ REVEALS Himself: Jesus Christ REDEEMS you: Jesus Christ enters into a RELATIONSHIP with all who call Him Lord. Lord, I am seeking the three R's today . . . reveal Yourself in the wonder and beauty around me . . . and as my Redeemer I pray for that close relationship which You promised.

*In Christ revealed I wait the glory due;*
*Redeemed, restored – my song is ever new.*

* * *

# 18th November

My dear brothers, take note of this: Everyone should be quick to listen, slow to speak and slow to become angry, for man's anger does not bring about the righteous life that God desires. Therefore, get rid of all moral filth and the evil that is so prevalent, and humbly accept the work planted in you, which can save you. Do not merely listen to the word, and so deceive yourselves. Do what it says. . . . the man who looks intently into the perfect law that gives freedom, and continues to do this, not forgetting what he has heard, but doing it – he will be blessed in what he does.

If anyone considers himself religious and yet does not keep a tight rein on his tongue, he deceives himself and his religion is worthless.

Religion that God our Father accepts as pure and faultless is this: to look after orphans and widows in their distress and to keep oneself from being polluted by the world.

James 1:19–27

* * *

# 19th November

To Him who loves us and has freed us from our sins by His blood . . . to Him be glory and power for ever and ever! Amen.

Revelation 1:6

Although Bishop Thomas Ken died in 1711 – getting on for three hundred years ago – we can still identify with his prayers. In fact it is totally misguided to look at 'old' thoughts and writings as being irrelevant to our present day. From Adam and Eve, the human nature and needs have remained constant: Bishop Ken blessed his Saviour for the ordinary things in life. Lord, remind me that I am ordinary and it is in the ordinary that I live – so gild my life with the extraordinary vision of Your everlasting care.

*Glory be to Thee, O Heavenly Father, for our being and preservation, health and strength, understanding and memory, friends and benefactors, and for all our abilities of mind and body. Glory be to Thee for our competent livelihood, for the advantages of our education, and for the guard which Thy holy angels keep over us.*

*Thoman Ken*

* * *

# 20th November

If there is no resurrection of the dead, then not even Christ has been raised . . .

1 Corinthians 15:13

Life is full of 'ifs'! But some people become haunted by their own personal 'ifs', they get so frightened of being hurt and of failure that they take on the attitude that if they don't try, then they won't fail, and thereby they give up on faith. Selwyn Hughes puts it like this: 'Fearful people live on the "if only" level. If only I could do this – or that – but since "if only" never comes to pass, they never accomplish what they would like to do and they finish up defeated, disillusioned and downcast. There are so many such people and they need not our condemnation, but our help.'

*If you will follow Jesus*
*You'll really find abundant life –*
*If you will follow Jesus*
*Step out in faith upon the way*
*And come and follow the Lord!*

*J. B. Hindley*

* * *

# 21st November

Stephen, full of the Holy Spirit, looked up to heaven and saw the glory of God . . .

Acts 7:55

In this vale of tears and woe, maybe you are passing through what someone once described as 'a glen of gloom'. Let me ask you to look up – look up from the valley, because if, and when you do, you will see bigger things above. . . . These are the tomorrows that are awaiting you. . . . These are the better days in store.

John Jackson

*Pardon for sin and a peace that endureth*
*Thy own dear presence to cheer and to guide:*
*Strength for today and bright hope for tomorrow*
*Blessings all mine with ten thousand beside!*

*Thoman O. Chisholm*

* * *

# 22nd November

For you know that it was not with perishable things. . . . that you were redeemed . . . , but with the precious blood of Christ.

1 Peter 1:18–19

In the spring of 1949, a young Korean student was preparing to attend an international Youth Rally in India. He wanted to take with him a new hymn so he approached the Dean of the College of Music at Yonsei Christian University in Seoul, Tai Jun Park, and asked him to write a hymn. And so in May 1949, a beautifully direct and simple hymn was born. It is quite amazing how many hymns have almost escaped composition – we can never know the extent to which people, and especially the young, have been moved to a greater longing for peace by reading or singing these words:

*The Saviour's precious blood has made all nations one.*
*United, let us praise this deed the Father's love has done.*
*In this sad world of war can peace be ever found?*
*Unless the love of Christ prevail*
*True peace will not abound.*

*Tai Jun Park*

* * *

# 23rd November

Even though I walk through the valley of the shadow of death, I will fear no evil, for You are with me . . .

Psalm 23:4

At the lowest point of my life I 'took off' to a desolate part of a national park. Driving there I came on thick fog which almost made me turn back but once I climbed out of the valleys and up onto the wide open moor the sun shone in a clear November sky. I left the car and walked to the highest point in view then sat looking back over the miles I had travelled. Down there in the valleys, the fog still hung in great swathes of white in the distance, and I knew that people in those valleys could not enjoy the sunshine I was then sitting in. Above me birds circled and glided out of sight and above both birds and me, a plane left its trail in the sky. That plane had come from one horizon and soon disappeared into the next – it made all things fall into place somehow . . . the fog-bound valleys, the clearer view and the varying degrees of higher vision . . . I knew God was still with me.

*Every valley shall be raised up, every mountain and hill made low; the rough ground shall become level, the rugged places a plain. And the glory of the Lord will be revealed and all mankind shall see it together.*

*Isaiah 40:4–5*

* * *

# 24th November

When he came to his senses, he said, 'I will set out and go back to my father . . .'

Luke 15:18

Going home when you have left it under a cloud is never easy. To some it is impossible – as the mounting numbers of teenagers gravitating into large cities illustrates. Yet every human being has an overwhelming urge to be 'at home' or to 'go home', to be loved and accepted. My prayer today is for any who are away from home, out of favour, homesick, yet with that black feeling that they can no longer go home. Lord, say to their hearts now 'come to your senses . . . go back to your home . . . love only waits to forgive and forget, home, weary wanderer – home! Don't wait any longer – go home now.'

*Through many dangers, toils and snares,*
*I have already come;*
*God's grace has brought me safe thus far*
*And He will lead me home.*

*John Newton*

* * *

# 25th November

What causes fights and quarrels among you? Don't they come from your desires that battle within you? You want something but don't get it.

You kill and covet, but you cannot have what you want. You quarrel and fight. You do not have, because you do not ask God. When you ask, you do not receive, because you ask with the wrong motives, that you may spend what you get on your pleasures.

Submit yourselves, then, to God. Resist the devil and he will flee from you. Come near to God and He will come near to you. Wash your hands, you sinners, and purify your hearts, you who are double-minded. Grieve, mourn and wail. Change your laughter to mourning and your joy to gloom. Humble yourselves before the Lord, and He will lift you up.

James 4:1–3, 7–10

* * *

## 26th November

Jesus said: 'What good is it for a man to gain the whole world and yet lose or forfeit his very self?'

Luke 9:24

There is so much truth in some of the old sayings that now and again it does no harm to trot them out, and here is one for today: 'God does not want extraordinary people who do extraordinary things nearly so much as He wants ordinary people who do ordinary things well.' When a person is amazingly successful that person soon loses ambition and excitement in things; in a life centred on success, money or privilege there is often found the greatest emptiness and hopelessness. Lord, temper my ambition with kindness, may my dearest possessions be friendships and my greatest achievement be to lead another to know Jesus as Saviour and Friend.

*When I survey the wondrous cross*
*On which the Prince of Glory died:*
*My richest gain I count but loss*
*And pour contempt on all my pride.*

*Isaac Watts*

* * *

## 27th November

I pray that you . . . may grasp how wide and long and high and deep is the love of Christ, and to know this love that surpasses knowledge.

Ephesians 3:19

Baron von Hugel was close to death when he dictated these words: 'What a happiness, what a joy it is to be quite sure that there is a God: . . . more real than the air around us, and the pollen of the flowers, and the flight of the birds, and the trials and the troubles and the needs of our little lives stimulated and enriched by the lives of creatures so different from ourselves, touching us continually all around: it is an assurance . . . or a reality, of THE Reality, strong and self-sufficing, of God.'

Baron von Hugel

*I know that my Redeemer lives!*
*What joy the blest assurance gives!*

*Samuel Medley*

* * *

# 28th November

He was despised and rejected by men, a man of sorrows, and familiar with suffering.

Isaiah 53:3

O God, bless those who are burdened with cares. . . . However hard their circumstances, help them to discern the truth and see that their lives can be changed through the love of Christ our Lord . . . when depression takes hold, encourage them with Your inner truths, so that they can know the fullness of life: Lord Jesus, You spoke to the world through Your own suffering and triumph; speak to us now through the sufferings and triumphs and hopes of our sisters and brothers.

Joyce Hastings

*All you that pass by – to Jesus draw nigh:*
*Your ransom and peace, Your surety He is –*
*Come, see if there ever was sorrow like His.*

*Charles Wesley*

* * *

# 29th November

Jesus said '. . . I was sick and in prison and you did not look after me . . .'

Matthew 25:43

When a member of the family is in hospital we trot along on our duty visit. When a loved one is in hospital we can't get to visit quick enough. When a stranger is in hospital we never think about hospital. Lord, it is so hard to come to terms with Your words that we are honouring and worshipping You when we serve others – whether we love them, like them, dislike them or don't even know them. I pray today for those who will visit hospitals and prisons – and I pray for myself too, that I may make opportunities to serve by slipping along to see someone . . . and if I begin with someone I know, it will be that much more less difficult when it comes to a stranger.

*Lord, give us Your spirit*
*Your spirit that is love . . .*
*Where there is pain*
*Let us be Your healing hands . . .*

*Sandy Hardyman*

* * *

# 30th November

May our Lord Jesus Christ Himself and God our Father, who loved us and by His grace gave us eternal encouragement and good hope, encourage your hearts . . .

2 Thessalonians 2:16

St Augustine said, 'Hope has two beautiful daughters – anger and courage.' A strange remark on the surface but a deeper look at that word 'hope' and it is obvious how these two emotions do spring from mother hope. We need anger at injustice and alongside that we need courage to stand up for what we believe otherwise our hopes can never be realised. Dreams do not come true unless we do something – when ordinary people care enough and pray deeply for their God-given Hope, then miracles happen.

*Our hope's for unification*
*Even in sleep it is our dream.*
*We offer even our lives*

*For the unity of our land –*
*Come to us, unification!*
*All people in this land wait for you.*
*Come now and heal our division*
*Unification come!*

*from Songs of the Minjung*
*Ecumenical Youth Council in Korea*

* * *

# 1st December

The Son is the radiance of God's glory and the exact representation of His being, sustaining all things by His powerful word.

Hebrews 1:3

If I love someone very much, there are many ways in which I can express that love – by an act of kindness, by a touch or a smile, but one of the most powerful means of conveying that love is by word of mouth (though even that is often inadequate). God is the great Lover. Because He is love, he is always seeking ways of communicating with His creatures. . . .

In human intercourse, a word spoken in love can be spurned or neglected. On the other hand, it can be heeded and received. It is so with God's Word Incarnate. Because God has spoken to us in His Son, the onus on ourselves is heavy.

Lord Coggan

*We must pay more careful attention, therefore, to what we have heard, so that we do not drift away. For if the message spoken by angels was binding, and every violation and disobedience received its just punishment, how shall we escape of we ignore such a great salvation?*

*Hebrews 2:1–3*

* * *

# 2nd December

In those days John the Baptist came, preaching in the Desert of Judea and saying, 'Repent, for the kingdom of heaven is near'. This is he who was spoken of through the prophet Isaiah:

'A voice of one calling in the desert, Prepare the way for the Lord – make straight paths for him!' John's clothes were made of camel's hair, and he had a leather belt around his waist. His food was locusts and wild honey. People went out to him from Jerusalem and all Judea and the whole region of the Jordan. Confessing their sins, they were baptised by him in the Jordan river.

'I baptise you with water for repentance. But after me will come one who is more powerful than I, whose sandals I am not fit to carry. He will be baptise you with the Holy Spirit and with fire.'

Matthew 3:1–11

* * *

# 3rd December

Jesus said: Peace I leave with you, my peace I give you.

John 14:27

*Come to the world!*
*Yes, God the Creator, come!*
*Things are not as you created them in the beginning.*
*Come, God, for it is your help we need in the world.*

*Peace of mind,*
*Yes, that's what everyone wants.*
*Our need, please God, is true peace in the world.*
*Peace of mind,*
*Yes, that's what everyone prays for.*

*What is the state in the world?*
*Come and see how our people are destroying the world,*
*Without seeking what is in Your heart*
*Without seeking what is in Your mind.*
*Come and see how retaliation prevails among us*
*Without fearing You,*
*Without recognising brotherhood.*
*Rise, brethren and live together,*
*Yes, if we seek peace, God will grant us peace.*

*Ikole Harcourt Whyte (Nigeria)*

Come to my heart Lord Jesus, Prince of Peace, Wonderful Counsellor Mighty God, . . . come to my heart with the peace that passes all earthly understanding.

* * *

# 4th December

Let us then approach the throne of grace with confidence, so that we may receive mercy and find grace to help us in our time of need.

Hebrews 4:16

People often say to me, 'You church people are always appealing for money, wanting to keep the institution going at all costs.' In their hearts they long for spiritual and moral support in the face of suffering, depression, death; they look for meaning in the changes and confusion of our time, in the temptations of materialism, unrestrained selfishness, failing standards. They want help in preserving family life, and compassion when marriages break down or when one partner dies. If people find the Church eager to support them in all the pressures and demands of life, they will support it . . . to continue this supporting work.

George Appleton
former Archbishop in Jerusalem

*He bids us build each other up*
*And, gathered into one,*
*To our high calling's glorious hope*
*We hand in hand go on.*

*Charles Wesley*

* * *

# 5th December

A wife of noble character is worth far more than rubies. . . . she opens her arms to the poor and extends her hands to the needy. . . .

Proverbs 31:10–20

As Christmas approaches I become so swept up in the commercial aspect of it that it's hard to retain the real meaning of it all. How many Christmas cards? Which parties to go to? More decorations? As a Christian, I am also torn by my plenty compared with the poverty of the Third World. . . . One day I poured my feelings out to God. . . . I sensed that God was telling me that He understood what I was going through. He showed me that if I bought my presents for each person lovingly, God would be pleased. If I prepared food for each occasion with love in my heart for each person who would be enjoying it, then God would receive my love too.

Fiona Castle

*Of her, Immanuel, the Christ was born. . . .*
*And Christian folk throughout the world will ever say*
*'Most highly favoured lady'.*
*Gloria!*

*Basque Carol*

* * *

# 6th December

The Word became flesh and lived for a while among us.

John 1:14

O God of truth, as you have given Your Word to men, so strengthen the hands of all who have a part in making it more widely known in our day. We pray for those engaged in the work of translation and production; for distributors and colporteurs; for teachers, pastors, and evangelists; that the timeless truth of the Bible may be communicated to men and speak to their needs in living language and with saving power; through Jesus Christ our Lord.

Contemporary Parish Prayers

*For Your holy book we thank You*
*May its message in our hearts*
*Lead us now to see in Jesus*
*All the grace Your Word imparts –*
*Steadfast love and tender care*
*For Your people everywhere.*

*Ruth Carter*

* * *

# 7th December

As Jesus approached Jerusalem and saw the city, He wept over it.

Luke 19:41

And I believe Jesus looks today on every city of the world and weeps – the poverty, the loneliness, the crime, abuse of children and ill-treatment of wives, the tears. . . .

Sheila Walsh wrote: 'If we spent as long on our knees weeping over our cities and towns as we do planning new methods of evangelism, I believe the spiritual temperature in our country would soar.' Lord forgive me that I don't care enough to be moved by people's circumstances. Today, I will kneel and remember. . . . give me the sympathy in my heart to put myself in their shoes . . . give me understanding and a longing for justice and peace of mind for all.

*Did Christ o'er sinner weep?*
*And shall our tears be dry?*
*Let floods of penitential grief*
*Burst forth from every eye.*

*B. Beddome*

* * *

# 8th December

Fathers, do not embitter your children, or they will become discouraged.

Colossians 3:21

Most parents face the temptation of expecting far too much of their children, in behaviour, in ability and achievement. Row upon row erupts because the children feel parents are for ever 'getting at' them and are not truly pleased with the child as a person just as they are. Lord, help me to see I cannot regain lost opportunities through my children, give me a warm heart to love them as they are – as You love me, warts and all! I pray that today my nagging will turn to words of encouragement, shouted commands become friendly banter and my harassed brow give way to a smile of thankfulness that I do have children to love.

*Children cannot control their world; they are dependent on those of us who care for them.*
*Children need us to nurture them so that someday they will be strong enough to sustain this ever-changing world.*
*Help me to love my family . . .*

*Judith Mattison*

* * *

# 9th December

For to us a child is born, to us a son is given, and the government will be on his shoulders. And He will be called Wonderful, Counsellor, Mighty God, Everlasting Father, Prince of Peace. Of the increase of His government and peace there will be no end.

He will reign on David's throne and over his kingdom, establishing and upholding it with justice and righteousness from that time on and for ever. The zeal of the Lord Almighty will accomplish this. . . .

A shoot will come up from the stump of Jesse; from his roots a Branch will bear fruit. The Spirit of the Lord will rest on Him . . . the Spirit of wisdom and understanding.

Isaiah 9:6–8 & 11:1–2

* * *

# 10th December

Jesus said: 'Come to me . . .'

Matthew 11:28

*You asked for my hands*
*that You might use them for Your purpose –*
*I gave them for a moment then withdrew them*
*for the work was hard.*

*You asked for my mouth*
*to speak out against injustice –*
*I gave You a whisper that I might not be accused.*

*You asked for my eyes*
*to see the pain of poverty.*
*I closed them for I did not want to see.*

*You asked for my life*
*that You might work through me.*
*I gave a small part that I might not get too involved.*

Lord, forgive me for my calculated efforts to serve You only when it is convenient for me to do so: only in those places where it is safe to do so, and only with those who make it easy to do so.

Joe Seremane
South Africa

* * *

# 11th December

Dear friends, let us love one another, because love comes from God. . . . Dear friends, if this is how God loved us, then we should love one another.

1 John 4:7 & 11

An expert on the 19th century reformer William Wilberforce said: 'The great thing about William Wilberforce was that he always kept his friends.' What a splendid tribute. In changing world and changing families it is often hard to keep in touch, difficult to make new friends – but this is a day to remember and to value true friendship. In all the card-sending of this Christmas may I add those special words for my friends, give that extra detail and time for a special friend – Lord, You gave Your son to be Redeemer and Friend to all and He knows the hurt of rejection and abandonment . . . forgive me.

*Lord, thank You for friends, for love, for laughter, for understanding. Thank you for friendships which stand the test of time, for friends to grow up with, to grow old with. Help us in our friendships to reflect Your love. Help us to love each other as You love us, and may You be the heart of all our friendship.*

*Margaret Cundiff*

* * *

# 12th December

'What have I to do with thee, O man of God?'
1 Kings 17:18–20

Dr Joseph Parker was a much admired and loved preacher – congregations looked up to him as a great man of faith. But when his beloved wife died, Dr Parker plunged into a terrible black doubt until he felt he had lost his faith altogether. With time his anguish passed and he realised God had not forsaken him, and with his deepened understanding and empathy with the needs of his listeners, he spoke with even more power than before. At some time or another we all go through a numb hell of doubt – our faith slips away and we turn only to rebuke God. Lord, loving Father, carry us through until our mourning turns into morning.

*Today Lord, I pray for those approaching Christmas who have suffered loss this past year and face the coming days with a heavy heart. Bless each troubled soul and give the comfort of a good night's sleep.*

* * *

# 13th December

A friend loves at all times

Proverbs 17:17

*Among the great and glorious gifts our heavenly Father sends*
*Is the gift of understanding that we find in loving friends. . . .*
*So when we need some sympathy or a friendly hand to touch,*
*Or an ear that listens tenderly and speaks words that mean so much,*
*We seek our true and trusted friend in the knowledge that we'll find*
*A heart that's sympathetic and an understanding mind.*
*And often just without a word there seems to be a union*
*Of thoughts and kindred feelings for God gives true friends communion.*

*Helen Steiner-Rice*

Jesus said: 'My command is this: love each other as I have loved you. Greater love has no one than this, that one lay down his life for his friends. You are my friends if you do what I command.'

John 15:12–14

* * *

# 14th December

The whole assembly bowed in worship, while the singers sang and the trumpeters played.

2 Chronicles 29:28

This is the season of carol singing! Groups of adults and children will be making the annual pilgrimage into hospitals, homes for the handicapped and elderly, and hospices. Dame Cicely Saunders, founder of the whole hospice movement, makes it plain how important carol singing can be: 'Every word of each carol matters to those who listen. . . . We are celebrating and singing to Love – the Love th welcomes everyone who has love to offer. We are singi to Love: love as given to us in our daily life through love of others, but given supremely in the life of Jesus

*Sing we the King who is coming to reign!*
*Hell hath no terrors and death hath no sting*
*Love is victorious when Jesus is King.*

*Charles Silvester Horne*

* * *

# 15th December

Those who are wise will shine like the brightness of the heavens, and those who lead many to righteousness, like the stars for ever and ever.

Daniel 12:3

I can still remember the elation of looking in my school book and seeing a *. The occasions were all too infrequent – as for most of us – so I suppose the moments of junior achievement stand out. To be given a star by the teacher was something special – and in the book of Daniel we read that people who are good examples, people who exert a calm and good influence on others stand out and shine like actual stars in the night sky. Lord help me to be positive – so fill me with Your peace that my influence will be confident and right in Your sight. Forgive me that the times I stand out against the crowd for 'righteousness' are as few as the stars I got in school . . . in the love of Jesus I will be stronger.

*In the strength of the Lord, let me labour and pray,*
*Let me watch as a winner of souls:*
*That bright stars may be mine in the glorious day*
*When His praise like the sea billow rolls.*

*E. E. Hewitt*

* * *

# 16th December

In the past, God spoke to our forefathers through the prophets at many times and in various ways, but in these last days He has spoken to us by His

Son, whom He appointed heir of all things, and through whom He made the universe. The Son is the radiance of God's glory and the exact representation of His being, sustaining all things by His powerful word. . . . and again, when God brings His firstborn into the world, He says: 'Let all God's angels worship Him.'

But about the Son He says, 'Your throne, O God, will last for ever and ever, and righteousness will be the sceptre of Your kingdom.' . . .

Hebrews 1:1–4, 6 & 8

* * *

# 17th December

. . . . the star they had seen in the east, went ahead of them until it stopped over the place where the child was.

Matthew 2:9

*Laid up for ever in the fields of heaven*
*There glows the image of the Bethlehem stable,*
*Fled to the Star which led the Wise men there.*
*To Thee be glory Carolling in anthem – in Thy great mystery*
*All worship is de Babeled,*
*The tongues are mingled as they reach Thine ear.*
*Sung in America or Mozambique or China.*
*And Thou wilt answer on the wing of prayer –*
*So they be seen as singing just one carol*
*Whose notes are rays that centre on the Star.*

*A. J. Seymour (Guyana)*

As Christmas time approaches so fast, I pray Lord that I shall indeed feel at one with Your worldwide family, my worldwide family, and may our songs rise to You in the harmony of love.

* * *

# 18th December

An angel of the Lord appeared to them (the shepherds) and the glory of the Lord shone around them, and they were terrified. But the angel said to them, 'Do not be afraid, for I bring you good news of great joy . . .'

Luke 2: 9–10

Charles Wesley the marathon hymn-writer was born on 18 December 1707. He began one of his hymns: Hark! How all the welkin rings! – Hardly surprising that the hymn didn't catch the public's imagination and it was pretty well a flop. Then years later someone altered the first line and sang the hymn to a tune composed by the great Mendelssohn. The new combination was an instant 'hit' and it's no exaggeration to say that the hymn has been in the Christmas Top Ten ever since.

*Hark! The herald angels sing*
*Glory to the new-born King.*
*Peace on earth, and mercy mild,*
*God and sinners reconciled.*
*Joyful all ye nations rise,*
*Join the triumph of the skies;*
*With the angelic host proclaim:*
*Christ is born in Bethlehem!*

*Charles Wesley*

* * *

# 19th December

When I was a child, I talked like a child, I thought like a child, I reasoned like a child. When I became a man I put childish ways behind me.

1 Corinthians 13:11

Lord . . . Help me to give a little of myself if only for an hour, to a neighbour who is alone. Let me give a gift to a child who is in need – help me to let the love that is in my family overflow where it can. As a child, I wished that it could be Christmas every day, and grown-ups laughed. But the love that came at Christmas is with us every day. So may your give to me be Christmas Love That I can share in every day of every season.

Frank Topping

*As your family Lord, see us here . . .*
*Fill our spirits Lord with Your love . . .*
*Make us faithful Lord to Your will . . .*
*As Your family Lord, see us here . . . see us here.*

*Anon*

* * *

# 20th December

Jesus said: 'I will not leave you as orphans . . . because I live you also will live.'

John 14:18

Merry Christmas! Happy Christmas! How hollow those words will feel in the hearts of the thousands who have this year faced the loss of a love one and approach their first Christmas without that beloved presence. Happy? Merry? In so many ways we are not prepared to grow up – we desperately want to cling to the Happy and the Merry whilst all the time God gives us Christ's coming to adore. And He who came to share in our worldly pain promised that He would never leave us alone, bereft of His Holy presence and comfort. I grow up – things change – life goes on – my Lord is here!

*They that love beyond the world cannot be separated by it. Death cannot kill what never dies. Nor can spirits ever be divided that love and live in the same divine principle, the root and record of their friendship. If absence be not death, neither is theirs.*

*Death is but crossing the world, as friends do the seas – they live in one another still.*

*William Penn*

* * *

# 21st December

> Pharoah said: 'Make the work harder for the men so that they keep working and pay no attention to lies.'
>
> Exodus 5:9

As I look around in these last frantic days before Christmas, I see people who have become slaves to public opinion – slaves in the kitchen – driven ever onward in the quest for more security, more responsibility, greater influence and prestige; people working so hard they have no time to pay any attention to Bethlehem. No time for Jesus Christ. How empty their success and how hollow their seasonal greetings. Wily old Pharoah knew the psychological advantage of keeping his slaves noses to the ground. Father of all, free us, slaves to the world, to look up and see Your nativity.

*I pray for those who don't have time to listen to the story of Christ's birth – for all those who are bound up in a self-imposed whirlpool of activity to save them from confronting the New Born King. Lord, I give You my time . . . work will always wait!*

* * *

# 22nd December

> When the shepherds had seen Him, they spread the word concerning what had been told them about this child . . .
>
> Luke 2:17

The shepherds knew so much more than the other people in Bethlehem . . . What did they do? They told everyone! Do we know more than those for whom Christmas means 'Jingle Bells' and Santa Clause, or who only prepare for Christmas by getting cards off at the right time. They are trying to do their yearly duty! Jesus' coming was a free gift to all of us. Let us be ready for that feast so that we can prepare others too. Let us do what the shepherds did, and tell everyone who will listen.

Corrie ten Boom

*And go tell everyone*
*The news that God's kingdom has come . . .*

*Alan T. Dale*

* * *

# 23rd December

In those days Ceasar Augustus issued a decree that a census should be taken of the entire Roman world. And everyone went to his own town to register. So Joseph also went up from the town of Nazareth in Galilee to Judea, to Bethlehem the town of David, because he belonged to the house and the line of David. He went there to register with Mary, who was pledged to be married to him and was expecting a child. While they were there, the time came for the baby to be born, and she gave birth to her firstborn son. She wrapped him in strips of cloth and placed him in a manger, because there was no room for them at the inn.

Luke 2:1–8

* * *

# 24th December

In the beginning God created the heavens and the earth . . . And God saw that it was good.

Genesis 1:1 & 10

On Christmas Eve 1968 three men were orbiting the moon: Frank Borman, Jim Lovell and Bill Anders. Down the radio waves to Mission Control that night they read the first ten verses from Genesis Chapter 1 and then they closed down saying: 'and from the crew of Apollo 8 we pause with good night, good luck, Merry Christmas and God bless all of you on the good earth.' It's now more than two decades on and this is another Christmas Eve – I pray that God will still bless this earth with all it's goodness and make me better for pausing to think on these things.

*It came upon the midnight clear*
*That glorious song of old,*
*From angels bending near the earth*
*To touch their harps of gold:*
*Peace on the earth, goodwill to men*
*From heaven's all gracious King.*
*The world in solemn stillness lay*
*To hear the angels sing.*

*Edmund H. Sears*

* * *

# 25th December

### A Song of the Incarnation

The grace of God has dawned upon the world
With healing for all mankind.
The people who walked in darkness have seen a great light:
Light has dawned upon us, dwellers in a land as dark as death.
For a baby has been born for us, a son given to us.
God is love; and His love was disclosed to us in this,
that He sent his only Son into the world to bring us life.
We know how generous our Lord Jesus Christ has been;
He was rich, yet for our sake became poor,
so that through His poverty you might become rich.
God has spoken to us in the Son
whom He has made heir to the whole universe.
The Word became flesh; He came to dwell among us
and we saw His glory, such glory as befits the Father's only Son
full of grace and truth.

Hymns and Psalms

* * *

# 26th December

As soon as Jesus was baptised . . . a voice from heaven said: 'This is my Son, whom I love; with Him I am well pleased.'

Matthew 3:16–17

Throughout Jesus' life it was with the hurting and the broken ones he chose to spend His time; and He was crucified among them at the end. So, if you feel a little weary, a little rushed, a little breathless at the manger, then take heart because this message is for you. Christmas speaks above all else to the poor and the homeless, the hungry, oppressed and friendless of our world. We must never let ourselves forget that, or our celebrations will be as false as Santa's whiskers. But it also speaks to those who are burdened in any way, whether with regrets for the past, heartache in the present, or foreboding for the future. God says to us: 'Be strong, fear not, for I am with you – I am for you – here is my Son to prove it!'

J. Barrie Shepherd

*For to us a child is born,*
*to us a son is given.*

*Isaiah 9:6*

* * *

# 27th December

In Him was life, and that Life was the Light of men.

John 1:4

*One day, God said, 'Let there be love'.*
*And a child was born whose name was Light.*
*'I am the light of the world', He said,*
*'If you follow me you shall not walk in darkness.'*
*By this light, humanity was liberated,*
*The blind received sight*
*And to the poor the Good News came.*

*Today we celebrate the light, celebrate the hope.*
*In unity and in diversity*
*Because the Light, the Cross, and the Heart,*
*For the shalom of the world.*
*Together we build the future in hope . . .*
*We celebrate the diversity, affirm our oneness*
*In Christ, the Light, in whom*
*There is no east or west, black or white*
*But one people of the technicolour world.*

*Hae-Jong Kim*

Lord, I pray for the light of Your love to shine through me in this Christmas-time and into the days ahead . . .

* * *

# 28th December

Surely God is my salvation; I will trust and not be afraid. The Lord, the Lord is my strength and my song.

Isaiah 12:2

A couple were flying back to Britain after their first trip to the United States of America. Through the early morning wisps of cloud they looked down on Land's End, a place they had been many times before and, being on the ground had viewed it as the end of the country. Now they saw it from a different angle – no longer the end, but the beginning of land . . . the beginning of coming home. With this in mind, the husband, Alfred Wood, said, 'There are experiences of life and death, which, viewed from one angle are an ending, but with God they hold the possibilities of wonderful new beginnings. With the Hymn writer, we can "Praise Him for all that is past and trust Him for all that's to come." '

*Lord, I will not be afraid of the year that lies ahead of me – show me that through my life there are situations which have many angles: keep me from becoming blinkered in outlook, keep me trusting . . . keep me singing.*

* * *

# 29th December

And now these three things remain: faith, hope and love. But the greatest of these is love.
1 Corinthians 13:13

*A loving person never loses patience with people,*
*is always at their service.*
*A loving person isn't envious of anyone,*
*or disrespectful towards anyone.*
*People who really love never boast,*
*never consider themselves more important than others,*
*and never do anything for selfish motives;*
*they don't take offence*
*or keep score of wrongs done to them.*
*A loving person doesn't revel in peoples' misdeeds*
*but only enjoys what is right and true.*
*A loving person forgives others without limit,*
*encourages them by placing confidence in them,*
*and never gives up hope in them.*
*Loving people is something that can never come to an end:*
*where everything else falls short*
*and when everyone else has given up,*
*the loving person still goes on loving.*

*John Hastings*

O, Lord God, help me to grow into a loving person . . .

* * *

# 30th December

This is how we know what love is. Jesus Christ laid down His life for us. And we ought to lay down our lives for our brothers. If anyone has material possessions and sees his brother in need but has no pity on him, how can the love of God be in him? Dear children, let us not love with words or tongue but with actions and in truth. This is then how we know that we belong to the truth, and how we set our hearts at rest in His presence whenever our hearts condemn us. For

God is greater than our hearts, and He knows everything . . . And this is His command; to believe in the name of His Son, Jesus Christ, and to love one another as he commanded us . . . And this is how we know He lives in us: we know it by the spirit He gave us.

1 John 3:16–24

* * *

# 31st December

Because You are my help I sing in the shadow of your wings; I stay close to You; Your right hand upholds me . . .

Psalm 63:7

It is much more the direction in which a man is going than the number of miles he has covered which matters. We can follow in the steps of the Master, and though we falter and stumble, He will call us by name, if, after each fall we struggle on again after Him. That's the Christian life, or better, the Christian adventure, and everybody can make it with God's help.

Lord Soper

*Thank You, Lord, for being my help through the past year:who knows what the next year holds, but whatever happens in the days ahead, I will stay close to You for my Christian adventure . . .*
*the prayer I breathe is*
*'All my hope on God is founded'.*

* * *

# People I want to remember in prayer

# Notes